CW00557820

THE
WEALTH
CREATORS

THE

WEALTH CREATORS

TOP PEOPLE, TOP TEAMS
& EXECUTIVE BEST PRACTICE

ANDREW KAKABADSE

**KOGAN
PAGE**

Disclaimer

The masculine pronoun has been used throughout this book. This stems from a desire to avoid ugly and cumbersome language, and no discrimination, prejudice or bias is intended.

First published in 1991

Apart from any fair dealing for the purposes of research or private study, or criticism or review, as permitted under the Copyright, Designs and Patents Act, 1988, this publication may only be reproduced, stored or transmitted, in any form or by any means, with the prior permission in writing of the publishers, or in the case of reprographic reproduction in accordance with the terms of licences issued by the Copyright Licensing Agency. Enquiries concerning reproduction outside those terms should be sent to the publishers at the undermentioned address:

Kogan Page Limited
120 Pentonville Road
London N1 9JN

© Andrew Kakabadse, 1991

British Library Cataloguing in Publication Data
A CIP record for this book is available from the British Library.

ISBN 0 7494 0373 X

Typeset by BookEns Ltd, Baldock, Herts
Printed and bound in Great Britain by
Biddles Ltd, Guildford and King's Lynn

Contents

Part III Sustaining Momentum

6

Acknowledgements

I would like to thank Paul Dainty, Siobhan Alderson, Andrew Myers and Mairi Bryce, all of whom played a major part in bringing the Top Executive Research Programme to fruition, so as to enable me to write this book. Their sharp insight, endeavour, patience and good humour have made it an extremely rewarding experience to have worked with such an enterprising team.

Thanks also to Sir John Hoskyns, ex-director-general of the Institute of Directors; John Nicholas and John Harper of the Institute of Directors; and Liam Gorman of the Irish Management Institute, whose support made it possible to conduct a wide-ranging and demanding survey.

My gratitude to Professors Leo Murray and Shaun Tyson, who afforded me the opportunity to undertake the research programme by lightening my administrative and teaching load at the Cranfield School of Management. My gratitude extends to Judith Gray, who, with such tolerance, typed and retyped draft after draft, always to a high standard and always with a smile.

A special mention for Carolyn Brunton, Godfrey Golzen, Tony Jackson, Donna Lucas and Ron Ludlow, who provided me with invaluable comment on the earlier drafts.

Finally, my special thanks to my wife Patricia and daughter Sophia for their willingness to make the time and space for my writing, in the full knowledge that I was encroaching upon something that we three deeply value – family time. In their own way, they wrote this book with me.

Preface

Over 60 per cent of business organisations are badly managed. Furthermore, 52 per cent of chairmen and CEOs (chief executive officers) of UK and Irish corporations feel uncomfortable about the effectiveness of the top team leading the organisation and the performance of its members. These latest survey findings make worrying results, especially as chairmen, CEOs and general managers are the ones making such comments.

A few years ago, I decided to focus my efforts on the training and development of top executives. Entering tentatively into this new arena of work and reading the research and wisdom of others, as well as learning on the job with my first few contracts, I became increasingly puzzled. An inordinate number of popularly written books, difficult-to-read books, and at times impossible-to-read research articles seemed to focus on one factor – the business leader.

- What are the characteristics of a successful business leader?

- What are the styles of successful business leaders?

- Have the styles of successful business leaders changed over the last two decades – from San Francisco, flower-power participative management to, now, a greater focus on product quality, sales and marketing, and a more directive style?

Interesting questions, but ones that did not entirely match my experience.

The more I dealt with top management, the more I recognised that the top team, *not* the successful business leader, should be the focus of analysis.

Just look at what's been happening in the business world over the last decade. Mergers, acquisitions, and organic growth, as well as emphasis on product quality, quality of service, customer care, managing, and responding to change, have been commonplace experiences of mid- to large-sized corporate organisations. The spectacular growth of Mercury Communications Ltd; the ever-growing success of Heinz, where current sales are over £6 billion worldwide; and the penetration of the North

American market by the Bank of Ireland, whose success in Ireland has continued in the UK, making it a player of some merit in the domestic mortgage market – what do these organisations share? Closer analysis reveals effective teamwork at the top. Lord Tombs, Chairman of Rolls Royce, and Colin Sharman of KPMG Peat Marwick McLintock would be the first to champion the importance of teamwork. So, too, would Tony O'Reilly, Chairman and Chief Executive of Heinz; Gordon Owen, Chairman of Mercury Communications Ltd and Group Managing Director of Cable and Wireless plc; and others too numerous to name.

What does the term *team* mean, especially when referring to top managers? It is abundantly clear to me that the term *team* means something far more than team styles or how to run meetings. Close observation indicates that the team running a business is the key unit by which meaningful business issues, such as sales and marketing, levels of costs required to induce the desired revenue streams, vision, organisation structure, team styles, people management styles, and how top managers should behave, are discussed and addressed.

Recently, however, greater attention has been given to the business leader, that influential individual who can introduce a new reality into the organisation. Certainly, it is easier to identify with one person than with a team, for, projecting the image of the hero – Richard Branson and Anita Roddick – or of the fallen hero, is much simpler than making a comparable popular impact with a team. What I learnt, however, is that it is the concept of team that drives the business, even though key individuals may have a powerful influence on the top team and the organisation.

Hence, I decided that I did not know enough. It was time to do some research. So, I consulted with, interviewed, counselled and surveyed over 1100 top managers representing over 740 organisations. As stated, certain startling results emerged. Over 60 per cent of UK and Irish businesses are badly managed. In particular, 63 per cent of general managers recognise that substantial problems exist in their top team which prevent the organisation from achieving its objectives. This is a damning statement which questions the capability of top management.

How has such information been gathered? The research programme covered two stages.

Stage 1

For 36 months, my research team and I became intimately involved, as consultants, with 36 separate organisations, some UK, some North American, four Irish, one Greek and three French. They included two police organisations, one local authority and two health service organisations. Apart from the public-sector organisations mentioned, the business organisations covered banks, high-tech companies, consultancy organisations, manufacturing organisations (consumer and industrial) and ones recently privatised. We observed a great deal and asked even more questions, such as the following.

- Are those who attain high office, a breed apart or just like anyone else?
- What does the term *vision* really mean?
- What is required to be a consistently successful top manager?
- What does it take to perform well as a top team and as the individual in the top team?
- In fact, who, and what, make up the top team?
- How can one recognise individuals who exhibit the potential for appointment to high office?

What this close scrutiny identified was a distinct and finite number of clusters of skills, in fact, *five*, necessary for the effective management and leadership of an organisation. What also emerged was the damage that could be inflicted on the overall organisation; on the function, team or department for which the individual executive is responsible; or on the executive himself, in terms of stress and frustration. In essence, this damage was above and beyond normal wear and tear, should these skill clusters be partly applied, badly applied or not applied at all.

Stage 2

Armed with such insights, we have completed an extensive survey of top managers and top teams in the UK and Ireland. The combination of personal experience and survey findings provide the data for this text. To add meaning to this book, we also have provided examples of the best practice in UK and non-UK organisations.

STRUCTURE OF THE BOOK

The book comprises seven chapters divided into three sections. At the end of each chapter is a summary of *best-practice* behaviour and approaches, which in combination lead to effective performance at the individual and team level, which is vital to the future success of the organisation.

11

The shaping skills

Chapters 1–3 are devoted to identifying the issues to be addressed and skills to be applied in three fundamentally important strategic areas:

Shaping the future   – vision – what vision means and how to implement vision

Shaping the team   – what is required in pulling together the people who run the business, in order to produce a high-performing top team

Shaping the business – what are the key concerns to be addressed in making the structure work

The influencing skills

Chapters 4–5 examine the key behaviours and practices required for the influencing of individuals and teams, so that a shared understanding of where the organisation is going and a commitment to its success, become deeply ingrained values, in staff and management alike.

Spreading the message – the skills and practices involved in effective communication are identified

Hearing what's said   – the skills and practices involved in listening and winning the commitment of others are examined

Sustaining momentum

Chapters 6–7 explore the actions that need to be applied in order to generate a culture of success within the business, while minimising the possibility of failure, and to develop executives in post as well as those who exhibit the potential for high office.

The success culture   – the approaches to maintaining and expanding a successful organisation are identified, with special emphasis on how to minimise damage to the organisation

Executive development – approaches to training and developing top managers in post as well as those who exhibit the potential for senior responsibilities are discussed

For the future, through sister institutions acting as enablers and facilitators, the research team and I will gain access to thousands of other top managers. In continental Europe, the survey will cover Sweden, Denmark, Finland, France, Germany, Austria, Spain and Italy. Negotiations are under way to proceed with the survey in Japan and the US. The Cranfield School of Management should shortly have one of the largest databases in the world on top executives, by industry type, size of organisation, nationality, age, attitudes and styles. The similarities and differences between top executives of different countries across different industries in terms of what is effective and ineffective individual and team performance, what success really means across the world, and what are the sources of failure will be the topics of the next book. However, what has clearly emerged is that the core competencies and skills required for the effective discharge of high office are unlikely to alter.

STYLE

The book is intentionally written in an easy-to-read, jargon-free style, suitably enriched by case studies and statements from those executives who agreed to be interviewed and quoted. Wherever possible with stories of success or successful practice, the executive is identified and his words highlighted. In this way, the reader can visualise the context in which the statements are made, adding a sense of colour and life.

In addition to colour and life, this book features the element of learning from failure, an element which adds a sense of down-to-earth reality. With stories of failure or poor practice, the identity of those executives involved is kept in confidence, as is the identity of their organisations. There is little need to identify the person who exhibits weaknesses or failings. Through failure, the point has been made.

FOR WHOM IS THIS BOOK INTENDED?

- For anyone concerned with building success into the organisation.
- For anyone concerned with making top class performance a way of life.
- For anyone concerned with the wealth creation process.
- For the aspiring executive aiming for the top.
- For the executive who is considering how a successful business can sustain momentum.
- For anyone not involved in the executive world who may have pondered over the question of what is really demanded of executives who generate opportunities and who can bring about success.

The book is as much a *down-to-earth* analysis of emerging best practice, as it is a *how-to* book for those who already are, or wish to become involved in, the wealth creation process.

Andrew Kakabadse
February 1991

Glossary of abbreviations and terms

CEO

Chief executive officer

Culture

The culture of an organisation refers to the sum of the shared attitudes, beliefs, myths and behaviours as held and displayed by staff and management. In fact, when the attitudes, feelings and behaviours of people within the organisation are so natural to them that they may even be unaware of the image they project or of their behaviour pattern, then that is when a culture is formed. In reality, the vast majority of organisations display more than one culture according to the structure of the organisation, its history and the predominant leadership style(s) practised by its top management.

Dotted-line relationship

A dotted-line relationship is one in which an individual is required to refer to another individual without having the authority to dictate actions. Dotted-line relationships highlight key linkage points in the organisation structure. The relationship is one of influence, but not one of command. How the two parties relate and how the relationship evolves depends as much on the styles, attitudes and personalities of the parties involved, as on the culture and ambience of the surrounding circumstances. (See also **Straight-line relationship.**)

Executive

The executive is the senior management group responsible for driving the business

15

forward. Who are and who are not in the executive varies from company to company. The executive could be perceived as the board, or as the board together with those senior managers who sit on key committees, or as the directors of the company and the level or levels of general management below.

GM   General manager

HR   Human resources

IMD   International Management Development Institute
PO Box 1059
CH-1001 Lausanne
Switzerland

INSEAD European Institute of Business Administration
Boulevard de Constance
77305 Fontainebleau Cedex
France

IT   Information technology

MD   Managing director

PR   Public relations

R & D Research and development

Straight-line relationship   A straight-line relationship is a boss/subordinate relationship. In effect, one individual has authority over another according to the requirements of the roles held. (See also **Dotted-line relationship**.)

VP   Vice president

PART I
SHAPING SKILLS

Q: *Why do not more UK companies have a dominant position in world markets?*

A: Because dominance has not actually been seen as part of the main vision of UK companies ... They have not taken a longer-term view and looked at how they are going to achieve and maintain world dominance.

Lord Henry Chilver,
Chairman,
ECC Group

1

Shaping the Future

The CEO of the 21st Century will have to be able to create strategic plans and know precisely how and when to initiate them.

21st Century Report
Korn Ferry and the Columbia Graduate School of Business, 1989

The Euro-Strategist . . . plans his/her company's strategy for conquering new European markets from the corporate centre.

The Search for the Euro-Executive
A Saxton Bampfylde International Special Report, 1989

VISION

Comments from two reports, commissioned by well-respected search consultants, highlight a prime area of competence required of senior executives, that of *vision*, or the capacity to shape the future.

We have taken our company from being a rather stodgy mid-performing, rather unromantic pickle and ketchup company, into a multi-dimensional, international corporation . . . both in terms of conceptual approaches to the food industry and nutrition in general . . . So if you ask me what my vision is for the future, it is to maintain the dominance that we have established over the past 10 years as one of the leading food innovators in the world.

Dr Tony O'Reilly,
Chairman, President and CEO,
H J Heinz Co

Once appointed to a role of strategic responsibility, each senior manager needs to form a view on the future of the organisation, or of its function, for which he will be held accountable. Certain top managers may foresee considerable political and socioeconomic changes and may have changed their organisation to meet such challenges. In contrast, others may wish to preserve the status quo, perceiving the organisation to be structurally, financially, product-, and human-resource-wise capable of meeting challenges. Time eventually tells who is right or wrong.

Not to form a view concerning the future and where and how to focus the organisation and resources is simply to court problems. The organisation or function for which the senior manager is responsible would, as a result, not be focused to achieve objectives, and resources would not be fully utilised, with the consequences of disarray, demoralisation of personnel, and eventual decline of the business.

If vision is so important, what is vision?

Vision is the capacity to identify and coherently project the appropriate medium-to-long-term direction the organisation should pursue. In effect, the senior manager needs to express clearly the mission, identity and objectives of the organisation. Vision involves an intricate coupling of creativity and pragmatism. Creativity is required to grasp and foresee the mission and identity of the organisation. Pragmatism provides that down-to-earth detailed view of the organisation, whereby one can realistically appreciate how to achieve objectives. Effective application of vision involves addressing four factors, namely the ability to make choices, knowledge of the business, understanding the differences between sales and marketing, and identifying and positively projecting the contribution of the Corporate Centre.

Making choices

One characteristic common to all senior managers, in both private and public-sector organisations, is *discretion*, that is, choice which allows the individual to identify and pursue the policies, strategies and directions that are deemed appropriate. (See Case Study 1.1.) All executives who hold general management responsibilities, be they GMs, CEOs, chairmen or directors, must make choices. The difference between the choice potential in the roles of chairman, CEO and GM is one of degree.

Case Study 1.1

THE WORK OF THE BIOSS UNIT

BIOSS, or the Brunel Institute of Organisation and Social Studies, Brunel University, Uxbridge, Middlesex, has undertaken considerable research on the topic of executive work. From the original, pioneering work of Elliot Jaques at the Glacier Metal Factory, which categorises work as *prescribed* (requiring that tasks be undertaken, leaving little to judgement) and *discretionary* (considerable judgement is required), further extensive study indicates that individuals who occupy roles with high levels of discretion must exercise considerable mental and personal skills, ie capacity, to be able effectively to exercise discretion.

Jaques and the BIOSS team developed the concept of *time span of discretion*, namely the amount of time required realistically to evaluate decisions made. Low levels of time-span discretion mean that a decision made can be evaluated shortly after, in hours or days. In effect, the decision and the tasks are not too complicated. In contrast, the highest level of ability is required to make, defend and implement decisions that are made several years before they bear fruit. The individual not only has to have faith in his judgement, but must exhibit the capacity to appreciate current and future issues, so as to focus the organisation on what he considers to be the most fruitful way forward.

The director of manufacturing/production needs to decide the shape of his function and its contribution to the overall organisation. In order to do so, the director needs to be sufficiently familiar with the other parts of the organisation to assess realistically what manufacturing should be doing.

A poor senior executive always stands out! As director of manufacturing, for example, he wants to manage only manufacturing – in reality, to be a manufacturing manager – as opposed to working towards inducing added–value performance from manufacturing through integrating the function with corporate objectives.

It is no surprise to report our observation of tense executive relationships, if one or more members of the top team holds a different view for the future from that of colleagues. Once a senior manager forms a view on current and future trends and how to focus his part of the organisation in particular directions, he is naturally committed to that view and may not easily give way to alternate viewpoints. To do so could be interpreted as an abdication of personal responsibility. The situation could become especially complicated in multinational/international organisations, where differences of view can occur between key teams in a complex structure and even between individuals in key teams (see splits of vision later in this chapter).

Knowing the business

Realistically appraising the future and recognising the necessary steps to take in order to enhance the fortunes of the organisation depend on having intimate knowledge of the organisation and the markets in which the business operates. The following are relevant questions:

- What is the shape and configuration of the customer base?
- What more is required further to penetrate existing customer bases?

- What is required to penetrate new customer bases?

- What are the needs of important supplier/distributors and how should such understanding be used to nurture further the relationship between them and the organisation?

- How prepared are the various functions/units in the organisation to improve performance?

- What level of support services and what levels of cost are required to induce the desired revenue streams?

These are some of the questions that senior managers ask in high-performing companies. The answer to these questions requires an understanding of, and access to, *details* about the business.

Intimacy with the business means forming a sufficiently detailed view of the expectations of customers, the behaviour of suppliers and competitors, the time necessary to stimulate appropriate levels of sales, the likely life cycle of products, and the degree of after-sales care desired, in order to form conclusions as to *the levels of cost required to induce the desired revenue streams*. To form a view on the size of the cost base to be carried, how the company should be structured, and its positioning in the market, the executive needs to be able to extrapolate from that detail *a view on ways forward*.

It is the ability to concern himself with relevant detail, and from that to extrapolate a realistic picture of what to do, when and for how long, recognising the discretionary boundaries of his role, that distinguishes a high-performing senior manager from a mediocre senior manager.

Case Study 1.2

THE GEORGE VASSILIOU STORY

Not many people in northern Europe will have heard of George Vassiliou. He is, however, quite a topic of conversation in the Mediterranean region.

George Vassiliou is the president of the republic of Cyprus.

George is not a long-standing professional politician. He has devoted most of his working life to being a consultant and businessman. George was educated in Hungary, and on returning to Cyprus in the 1960s started a small business in marketing consultancy. George's vision was that Cyprus could become an important services centre for the Middle East. By the 1980s that dream had turned into reality, as George's small business – MEMRB – had been shaped into one of the largest and most profitable service organisations on the island.

MEMRB – the Middle East Marketing Research Bureau – is not only an economic landmark, but also an aesthetic one, for the MEMRB building is one of the tallest and most impressive constructions in Nicosia.

In one sense, George is no different from anyone else. Most Cypriots are clever and intelligent traders. Cypriots, by nature, are people of business. Most Cypriots lost family, possessions and livelihood in the political turmoil and war of 1974. So did George.

In another sense, George stands apart from others. He was not content to be a success just in business; his political aspirations emerged in later life. In 1987, in his mid-50s and with no previous active political experience, George decided to stand for president. Against considerable odds, George was elected president of the republic within nine months. The team he formed around him to fight the campaign, the manner in which he orchestrated the team and the campaign, and his style of delegation, strongly suggest a man who holds the rare gifts of capacity for detail and creativity.

A year prior to the campaign, George completed a well-known psychometric test, commonly administered on executive development programmes. It was no surprise to discover that the man's psychological profile displayed a comfortable balance between being practical and comfortable with detail and a capacity for intuition and creativity. On seeing the results, George remarked, 'I knew I was not academically brilliant but I am sufficiently long term to know not only what to aim for but also how to do it.'

George is some way through his period of office. Political survival can be based on many vagaries, but it would be foolish to discount the possibility of his winning a second term in office.

It is from relevant detail that a vision for the future is formed. There is little point in attending creativity courses or playing chess, in the hope that such exercises enhance visionary capacity. The key is to know your business and what you want to do with your business or, for people such as George Vassiliou in Case Study 1.2, how to progress even further.

Knowing your sales and marketing

- What are the respective definitions of sales and marketing?
- What is the difference between sales and marketing?

A myriad of textbooks answer these questions clearly and succinctly, with the obvious conclusion that there is a difference between sales and marketing. Such a conclusion did not emerge from our case studies or survey.

Whatever executives may have reported concerning their sales and marketing practices, observation of their behaviour did not always support what they said. In fact, for businesses in the same industry, it became difficult to distinguish what one organisation reported as sales from what another reported as marketing, for the two practices seemed similar.

Table 1.1 Views of top managers on sales and marketing

Industry	Sales	Marketing
Manufacturing/Consumer	■ good relationship with customers ■ tailored to customer needs ■ trained salesforce ■ provide service ■ undermine competitor products at cheapest price ■ international outlook ■ induce customer perception of product quality ■ meet customer requirements ■ project value for money image	■ design, customer service ■ price ■ trained salesforce ■ after-sales service ■ quality ■ advertising internationally ■ technical service and engineering support leading to quality ■ customer requirement and service ■ image, good dealer network ■ customer satisfaction
Manufacturing/Industrial	■ timing of commodity price ■ long-term commitment in furious price-oriented market ■ competent salesforce ■ good after-sales service ■ expensive, direct, technical salesforce ■ technical relationship with customers; need to give advice	■ cost is key ■ differentiation from competition, reputation for service and quality ■ identification of appropriate customer targets ■ competent salesforce ■ advertising ■ competent market research ■ give impression of quality in all aspects of business ■ technical expertise/product development, quality ■ persistent contact with key clients
Merchandising	■ face-to-face contact ■ advertising awareness and image ■ marketing, research, telesales and external sales ■ price, cleanliness,	■ keeping in touch with our large existing customer base ■ large presence in the media and cold calling ■ dedicated personnel ■ price, convenience, location of retail outlets ■ good promotional

Industry	Sales	Marketing
	convenience and hours of operation ■ mail shots, advertising, referrals ■ quality of product and trust between customer and supplier	materials, press controls and exhibitions ■ quality of service and product ■ be competitive in the market place
Transportation	■ constant communication with customer base ■ individual tailoring of service package to clients ■ high-calibre, customer-oriented staff and consistency to ensure repeat business prevails ■ having cost-effective and efficient products designed to meet the client's needs ■ product demonstrations ■ delivery promises ■ competitive pricing	■ creation of constant awareness of company name and range ■ detailed comprehension of global markets ■ comprehensive client-service requirements ■ customer perceptions of high standards of quality, service and cleanliness to ensure repeat business prevails ■ effective market network ■ public relations ■ identifying client needs ■ advertising, media and exhibitions
Financial	■ gaining confidence of clients ■ offering better terms/prices/products than competitors ■ establishing a relationship with the client ■ breaking customer resistance ■ expertise, quality and range; professionalism; objectivity and innovation	■ client contact ■ understanding client's needs ■ professional advice ■ targeting clients ■ presenting a professional image ■ TV advertising to ensure customer awareness ■ large, strong salesteam ■ well-targeted services ■ manpower planning; good image ■ strong research and development
Publishing	■ quality service to existing customers	■ continuing to improve the products

Industry	Sales	Marketing
	■ highly trained and motivated salesforce capable of digging deeper into market potential ■ basic prospecting ■ expertise ■ a network of profes-sional staff ■ good mailing lists; well-produced materials ■ carefully targeted products	■ improving the quality and productivity of our sales performance ■ customer service ■ salesmanship ■ knowledge ■ targeted mailing lists ■ high reputation in the sector concerned
Management consulting	■ convincing customer he needs to be trained and we are the group to do it ■ hard work ■ quality of product ■ persistence in new markets, pricing, quality of delivery and backup ■ understanding bottom-line needs of clients ■ presentation skills and understanding of client's business	■ locals who know the market must be used and products customised for that market ■ publicity ■ persistence, personality, persuasiveness of product ■ visibility in marketplace; personal contact with potential clients ■ professional but uncomplicated approach; sympathetic attitude ■ contacts and business awareness

Table 1.1 summarises the comments made by respondents to describe their approaches to the sales and marketing of their products and services. The overlap in meanings is considerable. Terms such as price, design, customer service, customer satisfaction, support, image, trained sales-force, and even advertising appear in both columns, irrespective of indus-try type. There is no hard-and-fast rule as to what sales and marketing mean. Sales and marketing are interpreted differently in different organisations according to the circumstances and needs of each business.

What is important is that the *distinction* between sales and marketing, as applied to a particular organisation, is *understood* by the members of the top team and that the *commitment* exists to apply consistently such a distinction in the running of the business.

In one organisation, the comments shown in Case Study 1.3 were made by certain members of the top team regarding sales and marketing practices for their organisation.

Case Study 1.3

COMPANY X – HI-TECH COMMUNICATIONS

In interview, comments were made by the top-team members of company X, as to what they perceived their approaches to sales and marketing to be.

Sales	*Marketing*
■ A complete understanding of customer needs; system flexibility to respond rapidly to those changing needs.	■ A well-trained salesforce that understands how our products can lower customer costs.
■ Customer and salesforce education.	■ Varies from simply reviewing annual contracts to customer turnover.
■ Listening to the marketplace.	■ Identification of decision maker; thorough understanding of the product.
■ A mixture of carefully managed PR activity mixed with selective direct mail.	■ Educating our market to new ways of doing business.
■ Recognition that our company can provide high-quality services.	■ A large salesforce.
■ A good-quality trained salesforce capable of acting in a consultancy role.	■ Identify customer needs; professional selling skills.

Although there exists a certain overlap in meaning, closer discussion indicated that differences of view existed among senior managers as to the utilisation of the salesforce. The salesforces reported to the regional GMs. A small headquarters marketing team reported directly to the sales and marketing director. However, the sales and marketing director at corporate headquarters behaved as if he had a straight-line relationship with the sales managers in the regions, as opposed to the official dotted-line relationship. In effect, the sales and marketing director had to liaise with the regional sales managers. Instead, he tried to tell them what to do! Tensions existed between the sales and marketing director and the GMs, for in addressing issues such as meeting customer needs, PR, and adjusting the product portfolio to meet local requirements, the director missed out the GMs in his communications with the sales managers. Tensions led to bitterness, lack of communication, and inconsistency of application of policy. The persistent intervention of the CEO to appease the situation did not help. Finally, the CEO dismissed the sales and marketing director.

> As time passed, the sales and marketing director's vision as to developments in the marketplace and where to focus attention proved to be accurate. His mistake was that he alienated the regions.
>
> Whatever marketing and sales may have meant in business terms for that company, the implementation of marketing and sales meant nurturing positive and enabling dotted-line relationships with the regions, which, unfortunately, the sales and marketing director had not been prepared to service.

At the time of the marketing/sales director's appointment, no one, not even the GMs, had foreseen the crucial importance of managing marketing and sales through dotted-line relationships. In that company, marketing and sales were evolving concepts which could flourish only through the positive management of a sophisticated structure. Key managers needed to talk to each other as colleagues, not as superiors directing subordinates.

Getting the sales and marketing wrong has been the undoing of quite a few, including the rich and famous.

> It was all right while Sir Phil was able to run it hands-on, but once it started making acquisitions, the management did not seem to be able to get behind the marketing and selling properly.
>
> James Gulliver, on Harris Queensway, at the time of the £450m
> takeover bid.
> *The Times*, Thursday, 7 July 1988, p 25.

In well-managed businesses, such confusion of meaning does not occur. The senior managers of the organisation appreciate what sales and marketing mean for them, because time, energy and discussion have been devoted to these topics. What activities are to be placed in each function, how the linkages between the functions are to be managed, and how to address tensions in the structure will have been discussed, despite internal sensitivities. Even when the two functions report to one person, namely the sales and marketing director, the same issues have been observed to apply. Having one or two heads of function does not alter the debate as to what the shape, size and contribution of each should be for the effective performance of the business.

> Q: *What would the concepts of sales and marketing mean for your company? Is there a difference between the two?*
>
> A: Very clearly, yes . . . I don't see one as superior to the other. If you have a great marketing system and great creativity and a poor order-service and distribution system, the marketing men are going to want to go elsewhere.

Q: *What happens, do you think, when that differentiation isn't there?*

A: You get commodity trading.

Q: *And the business implications of that?*

A: Are lower margins and profits!

> Dr Tony O'Reilly,
> Chairman, President and CEO,
> HJ Heinz Co

Everyone has heard of Heinz – beanz meanz Heinz, if nothing else – and most know of Tony O'Reilly. Heinz and O'Reilly are now household terms, synonymous with success. One of the reasons for Heinz's success is the clear understanding of what sales and marketing mean for the company.

Detailed understanding of the concepts of sales and marketing and their application to your business are prerequisite to making vision work.

> What I try to do in my role is make the company into a sales-oriented company . . . We live or die by the sales we get through the door . . . We are gearing everybody up not just to be a salesperson, but to understand the sales side so they can support the sales initiatives and to make everybody realise that everybody in the company could seek out sales opportunities.

> Ken Cusack,
> MD, Sorbus UK

Sorbus is a computer-maintenance company, a wholly owned subsidiary of Bell Atlantic, in which quality of service and professionalism go hand-in-hand. The company's philosophy is clear – it is sales. For Ken Cusack, all staff and management need to understand the sales process. Engineers undergo sales training. According to Ken Cusack, 'Every time an engineer goes out on a chargeable job where the customer is not under contract, that is an opportunity to get a contract'. Sales training, sales-incentive schemes, and structuring the organisation for sales are key elements in the distinct and positive culture of Sorbus.

The reason that effectively managed businesses differentiate between sales and marketing is that they know they are not talking about techniques, but of culture, of a state of mind.

Case Study 1.4

THE SALES AND MARKETING OF BUSINESS SCHOOLS

What is the difference between the university-based and the more independent business/management schools?

Probably little.

The university-based schools such as London, Manchester, Cranfield, Bradford, and Strathclyde tend to offer the same array of management education and management development programmes as the independent schools of Henley and Ashridge. In fact, not just concerning executive-development programmes, but in terms of degree courses, Henley and Ashridge both offer MBA programmes as a result of their close relationship with university-based institutions. Close scrutiny of the major schools in the UK or even the two international schools in Europe, INSEAD in Paris, and IMD in Lausanne, would probably reveal considerably different practices as to the sales and marketing of their educational services. Cranfield tends to emphasise its management-development expertise, whereas some of the other schools are better known for their academic contribution.

What if, however, one of the schools wanted to make itself market leader? What would sales and marketing mean under those circumstances? Selling could mean sending out brochures, advertising, expanding and keeping up to date the client database, entertaining, and discussing client needs – in essence, all the current sales and marketing activities of the business schools would be seen as selling.

Marketing could mean the 'marketing of know-how'! For example, what if the director and his top team, especially of one of the university-based schools, decided to market the school as expert in five key areas of business and management, and, in order to achieve that status, identified five key research projects to be undertaken? What if the top team stipulated that the five most senior and competent academics should head each of the research projects, hence providing status and expertise to the studies? On completion of the studies, the results would be published only in those key journals popular with the fee-paying punters. What would the reaction of the academic body be?

Probably the reaction would be negative. Certain of the faculty would be openly critical of the senior management, accusing it of being heavy-handed. Others might come out in open rebellion, basically stating that the reason they entered university life was for the freedom to teach and research in their own way. Arguments centring on the increased revenue probably resulting from substantial investment in R & D, and on the reduced workloads resulting from focusing on particular customer groups, would do little to alleviate the probably adverse reaction.

Rethinking sales and marketing, even though considerable business advantages may be gained, without considering the culture of the organisation, or the key players in the organisation, is asking for trouble.

In business schools, as anywhere else (see Case Study 1.4 opposite), the culture, the history and the people in each organisation are unique to that organisation. So, in turn, are an organisation's approaches to sales and marketing, which, in turn, influence the way the company is structured and hence managed. Coopers & Lybrand Deloitte is as different from Price Waterhouse, as it is from KPMG Peat Marwick; AT&T is as different from Northern Telecom, as both are from Ericsson. The difference is qualitative. That qualitative element, when well managed, provides the competitive edge between an organisation that offers products and services that are recognised as sound, and one that induces 'added value' from its product-and-services portfolio.

It matters little that a mix of meanings over the terms *sales* and *marketing* occurs throughout businesses, even in the same industry. What counts is that the top-team members are clear and committed to what they mean by sales and marketing. It is imperative that each member of the top team, be he director of personnel or vice-president of manufacturing, holds an opinion as to the objectives, shape and identity of the sales and marketing function(s).

The survey results indicate that the only significant statistical relationship between the marketing and selling of products/services and other significant business performance factors, such as size and structure of organisation, morale of employees, market penetration, or cost control, is the attitude held by the members of the top team towards each other and towards the effective running of the organisation. The more positive the attitude of the top team, the more open the dialogue between the members of the top team, the more focused the sales and marketing strategies of the organisation.

It is worth investing time to discuss meaningfully the current and future sales and marketing philosophies and practices desired, no matter how initially tedious or irrelevant such conversation may seem. Once into such discourse, the surprise may be the difference of assumption as to what sales and marketing are or should be, as expressed by other senior managers. Senior teams not used to such conversations are likely to feel threatened, as differences of view are slowly teased out, and the implications for continuing with such differences are realised.

Contribution of the corporate centre

I'm tired of it! I'm tired of this Executive Board not working as it should. When it comes down to it, I could run those two of the five groups better than the two executive directors who are there. You keep telling me to get the team to work better – how? I know more

about sales and marketing than those two. The only way to do
things is to do them on a one to one.

Group CEO

Yes, but look – we all know you know the business; you've grown so
much a part of it! But now the problem is making the corporate
structure work.

Group finance director

I recently heard such a conversation. The group CEO of a large corporate
retail organisation in the US was convinced that two executive directors
responsible for two major parts of the group's business were incapable of
obtaining the results required. The group finance director, however, was
more in sympathy with his executive director colleagues, who felt themselves utterly constrained by the attitude and what they saw as the
erratic behaviour of the group CEO. The two executive directors in question
were the interface between group-level management and the MDs of the
operating companies. The two executive directors were finding it especially
difficult to project what added value the corporate centre offered to the
operating companies. As can be seen, this particular corporation was facing
problems. One of the operating company MDs had spoken out against
the corporate centres as 'the unhelpful element of the cost base'. The
group CEO had seriously considered firing the erstwhile and outspoken
MD, but was too concerned with damage to the image of the group that
might result, internally and externally, should such action be taken.
What the contribution of the corporate centre is to the shaping of the
future of the organisation is a crucial question to address for those corporate companies that have a diverse business base and/or a regional
structure, and that have grown to a substantial size.

Issues of sales and marketing are not the predominant concern of
corporate headquarters management. In order effectively to lead an
organisation with a diverse business base, a divisionalised configuration
should be adopted (see Chapter 3 on divisionalised structures). The
corporate centre's vision for the future is expressed in the continuing relationship with the operating companies. As a poor understanding of sales
and marketing is indicative of poor vision at operating company level, so,
too, at corporate centre level, vision, or the lack of it, is expressed by the
degree of commitment, identity or disaffection at the interface between
corporate centre and the operating businesses. There needs to be a clear
and shared view as to the contribution of corporate centre, within the
executive, in order for there to be clarity in questions of shaping the
future.

The corporate centre has to consider three key issues in its relationship with the operating businesses.

Group profile and strategy

What is to be the shape of the group? In which markets is the group to have a presence? What profile is the group to project, externally, to the market, press and financial analysts, and, internally, to its own management? Such are the issues facing Groupe Bull, France's state-owned, currently loss-making computer group, which has unveiled its restructuring plans designed to restore profitability by 1992. Starting from a Fr 1.88 billion loss in the first six months of 1990, the restructuring includes job losses in both the US and Europe, a reorganisation of production management, a rationalisation of plants, and the possibility of collaborating with competitors and big customers. Groupe Bull is clear! Where the company feels it cannot compete as a world leader, it will spin off parts of the business or enter into joint ventures, as it had started to do with Francois-Charles Oberthur, the French magnetic-card producer. Francis Lorentz, the chairman of Groupe Bull, is changing the profile of the corporation from that of a hardware manufacturer to that of a systems integrator, with the capability of bringing together hardware and software from different sources in order fully to address the customers' computing problems. In order to achieve such integration and focus, Bull's diversity of computer designs needs to be harmonised into a single product range. Hence, the need for cutting costs and plants, reducing staff, and rationalising administration, R & D, product design, and manufacture and sales.

Certainly, the need for a more sharply focused and improved quality of service to customers, spurred on by considerable losses, was one reason for Bull's restructuring. Another is that Bull, like other large producers, is a victim of the turbulence in the computer industry. Fundamentally, the market is now less favourable to traditional mainframes which offer producers substantial gross profit margins. The emphasis now is on low-cost, personal, computer-based systems, where margins are slim. In conversation, a number of senior Bull managers said that the need to improve was linked with consideration of the Japanese acquisition of ICL. Apart from anything else, something had to be done by Bull to prevent takeover.

Considerations of group profile and strategy can be driven by any of the following factors.

■ Economic and/or societal development reasons. A great deal depends on the views of the members of the corporate executive and their degree of mutual understanding and cohesion regarding the interpretation of external events and the future of the organisation.

33

- Market positioning reasons, either in terms of foreseeing future problems and introducing change before problems arise, or because by entering into new markets, the gains either financial or in enhancement of the profile of the group, would be improved.

- Rationalisation reasons. The group could have become so diverse, that all sense of group identity is being eroded, leading to costs being duplicated in the operating companies/affiliates, largely because central services cannot respond sensitively or quickly enough to such diverse demand. Accompanying increases in costs with diversity is the possibility of demoralisation. General management sees the corporate centre as inhibiting initiative, largely because the corporate executive at the centre has no understanding of the business, sales and marketing issues of the operating companies. Hence, operating company managers say that they experience inappropriate direction and an unhelpful dialogue with corporate headquarters. Identifying clear strategies forward has to be accompanied by establishing an open dialogue at the linkage points between corporate headquarters and the operating companies.

Corporate image

What values, qualities and identity are represented or should be represented by the corporate centre? Business values and their communication are discussed in detail in Chapter 4. However, an element of vision, that of projecting a particular corporate identity, can make a crucial impact on shareholders, financial institutions, analysts and customer groups as to the stature and viability of the organisation.

Such is the debate within KPMG Peat Marwick McLintock. In projecting a clear identity to the marketplace, what should Peats call itself? Created in its present form in 1987, by the merger of Peat Marwick Mitchel and KMG Thomson McLintock, the firm is not simply facing a branding problem. Like all of the big six accountancy/consultancy firms, KPMG Peat Marwick is not a wholly international business entity. It is a number of practices that collaborate on projects of mutual international concern such as training, investment, and quality care and enhancement, and that attempt to address the issue of overlap when dealing with international clients. In contrast, Hanson plc is strong in promoting the corporate name to enhance its standing with the investment community but downplays the holding company name as far as the sale of products is concerned – the operating company is emphasised.

What's in a name? The question of identity and image is an important concern for Peats. At a recent internal conference, it was highlighted how difficult it is to distinguish between corporate image and operating practice identity, for three reasons. Firstly, Peats does rely on local goodwill built on a track record of excellence of service. Secondly, the shape of the business is changing, as virtually 50 per cent of the firm's revenue is no longer audit based. KPMG is no longer an accountancy firm, but one which provides advice across a range of services. Thirdly, with international clients who, for example, may wish to investigate merger and acquisition possibilities overseas, whom do they choose? – the local office they know or the overseas practice which has KPMG in front of its name, such as KPMG Deutsche Treuhand (Germany) or KPMG Bohlins (Sweden).

The question of name – is an important issue to air, for the different views on the contribution of the corporate centre are thus allowed to emerge. The meaning of name for KPMG Peat Marwick, as an issue, has arisen from growth and success; success in expanding the consultancy side of the business; success in practising local networks; success in capability to service multinational clients with international aims. The issue of name is an important challenge for Peats in the shaping of its future.

The debate within Peats concerning corporate identity displays a healthy attitude to managing the future. This contrasts sharply with the corporate identity tensions that exist in the retail industry in the UK. What the perceived value of the corporate centre is, is a sensitive issue in certain retail organisations. Unlike KPMG, the issue of name is rarely, if ever, discussed.

Financial centre

How does the corporate centre address issues of financial contribution from the operating companies? To what extent does the centre truly appreciate the nature of the business of the operating companies when, through dialogue or through requirement, a level of financial contribution is targeted? To what extent does the centre justify or explain its role to the operating companies when certain levels of revenue are required?

It should be remembered that the corporate centre does not generate revenue. The operating companies make money! The corporate centre's key contribution is to examine the array of operating companies/affiliates to see which fit with group policy and strategy. Hence, motivating the operating businesses to contribute financially to a constantly evolving group profile is a process potentially fraught with tension. Why should the operating companies be inclined to provide greater financial contribution to the centre, unless they can recognise how they, in turn, benefit. In other words, is the centre little more than a bank?

Enabling contribution

For the corporate centre, the issues of the profile of the group and its future strategy, image and financial relationship with the operating businesses form the elements of the vision for the future. In order effectively to shape the future, a constructive dialogue needs to be established between the centre and the operating businesses. Both the dialogue and the ensuing relationship must be perceived as enabling by both the centre and the operating businesses. The purpose behind BP's recent restructuring is not only to reduce central costs and to achieve greater focus for the operating companies, but also for the centre to spearhead a new philosophy concerning quality of service and managerial practice for the future. For BP, crucial to achieving such a vision is the positive nature of the relationship between the centre and the operating businesses. This has been a prime concern of the specialist strategy and human-resource-planning groups within BP, as their aim is to stimulate a meaningful corporate identity at the centre and a positive dialogue with the operating companies.

It is important to identify what the centre is there to do! It could be active in determining the group profile, and in financial strategy, but could downplay the projection of a particular corporate image. Equally, the centre could behave more like a bank, concerning itself principally with investment decisions and the financial performance of the operating companies. Displaying a consistent identity will substantially enhance the relationship between the centre and the operating companies. The operating companies will clearly know what is required of them.

Hence, trust of the top management of the operating companies by the corporate executive, an open dialogue, and respect are as crucial to making visions work as is analytically identifying the strategies for the future. The sensitivities required for interfacing are as much a part of shaping the future as is establishing direction for the future.

Research strongly suggests that the experience of managing from the corporate centre is considerably different from managing in the operating companies. One top manager described the experience as managing by being one step away from reality. A considerable number of top managers did not relish remaining within the centre as they feared that they were getting out of touch and too involved in politics.

Whatever the problems of managing from the centre may be, it is the centre that needs to determine the relationship with the operating businesses. The centre enhances the relationship and dialogue. The operating businesses respond. There is no point in any of the following:

- the centre complaining about the poor performance of one or more of the operating businesses – either understand their problems and provide assistance or sell that business!

- the group CEO or any of the group executive thinking that he could do a better job in directly managing any of the operating businesses – he may be able to, but all that shows is how much he has *not* matured as a corporate top manager!

- complaining about the unhelpful attitude of the operating businesses – the businesses may not recognise or identify with the contribution of the corporate centre. All they see are expensive costs to which they are required to contribute!

- becoming frustrated with a poor-quality or even hostile dialogue with the operating companies – the centre sets the pace, so it's up to the corporate executive, preferably the group CEO, to confront such issues, even though such confrontation may induce emotions of considerable discomfort!

If poor performance at operating-company level or sensitivity at the interface(s) between the centre and the operating businesses persists, then the fault lies clearly with the centre. Either the centre is unclear as to what it contributes, or it is seen as too expensive, or it has not projected itself clearly enough, or personal sensitivities disrupt the dialogue. In corporate/divisionally structured businesses, the centre is required to shape the group's future as much as it is required to determine the dialogue with the operating businesses. Problems of vision in corporate organisations reflect the inhibitions and lack of clarity at the centre concerning the future as much as anything else.

SPLITS OF VISION

For the individual top manager to form a view as to how to shape and direct the future, is one issue. Clarity and coherence of view and commitment to that view at a team level are what counts. In mid-to-large-sized corporates, vision and its successful implementation is a team phenomenon, which requires time and attention in order to ensure a shared understanding by the members of that team as to the appropriate ways forward.

What happens if such shared understanding is not achieved? What happens if different views are held by the members of the senior team as to the future direction of the company? A considerable number of respondents indicated that different views on the direction of the company are held by the senior managers of their organisation. In fact, 38 per cent of the respondents emphasised that deep differences of view, concerning the future shape and identity of their organisation, existed within the top team. It is worth examining the implications of such splits.

Three distinct factors emerge from analysis, namely, poor management of the organisation, declining business performance, and morale problems with employees.

If the members of the top team are divided as to the future direction of the company, problems arise. The functional/divisional/corporate objectives of the organisation are not clearly defined or communicated. The result is that lower and middle managers' knowledge of the structure or who are the key top managers, is inadequate. Not surprisingly, the organisation is seen as poorly structured and requiring improvement. Reorganisations are perceived as poorly planned and implemented. Overall, the manner in which the functions/departments are run and the relationship between them require attention. At a more operational level, other problems occur. Poor understanding of the structure and poor interrelationships within the structure can lead to poor internal controls and hence wastage. Within such an environment, rules, procedures and guidelines tend not to be respected.

Significant trends emerge in terms of the performance of the organisation in the marketplace. Making changes to the company's products or services is poorly managed. The changes may have been insufficiently thought through, with the result that the investments made do not generate the desired revenues. Alternatively, the new products or services may be right for the market, but the change process from the old to the new product portfolios may have been poorly managed. Hence, staff may not understand or identify with the new products or services, with the end result that the business push required for improved sales is not forthcoming. Problems with the product portfolio may be symptomatic of more deeply rooted problems in the areas of sales and marketing. As discussed, the concepts of sales and marketing may not have been clearly thought through, resulting in poor focus on key customer groups, an inadequate ability to deliver goods/services or commitments made to customers on time, and a poor nurturing of key external relationships. The frictions within the top team extend and damage the business wisdom of managers lower down the organisation. As there is little pride in performing well externally, discussions concerning the competition and that natural on-the-job learning of where you stand in the marketplace are severely curtailed. After a while, managers either do not know how to or just do not meaningfully discuss what is happening *out there*! Hence, management's ability to respond to new initiatives, or simply its ability to cope with developments in the marketplace diminishes.

Inevitably, the larger the organisation, the more difficult it is to generate effective internal communications; identify clear structures; establish clear roles, responsibilities, and goals; and reduce wastage by improving the internal control systems. In mid-to-large-sized corporations, splits within the top team are much more apparent and the impact much more obvious. Those most likely to show discontent are the GMs (see Chapter 4). It is the GMs who have to implement vision. If they do not identify with the vision and policies put forward or find them suspect and poorly thought through, implementation of the vision through agreed strategies is inconsistent and incoherently communicated. Different and conflicting messages will emanate from senior management as to what needs to be done and why.

Fundamental disagreements on vision or the strategies required to accomplish particular ends inevitably surface as interpersonal problems – tensions within top management that are difficult to keep quiet. Splits and divisions among the members of the top team also affect the everyday management of the organisation. To the senior managers themselves, it is often clear that their team is perceived as unreliable in implementing what has been agreed. This leads to further blaming and resenting of each other, straining an already poor set of relationships.

Whether as a result of strained relationships or as a cause of them, the team members tend to identify with the function/department for which they are accountable rather than with the body corporate. Emphasis on functional performance reduces the chances of discussing cross-linkages and sharing of resources across the organisation. Eventually, the lack of discussion of fundamental corporate concerns potentially diminishes each individual's awareness as to the range and depth of corporate issues that need attention. It is no surprise to find that businesses in trouble have a senior management which still does not know 'what all the fuss is about'!

'What's the problem?' is a disturbing question, for it can highlight a dangerous lack of insight as to the nature and cause of the organisation's difficulties. Little surprise that the GMs at the receiving end of poor vision and mismanagement express concern.

For the rest of the organisation, lack of trust in the ability of top management to deliver grows. Within such an environment, the basic disciplines of management are given lip service. Attendance at meetings is sporadic. Meetings are changed at the 'drop of a hat'. Follow-through on commitments made is poor. Commitments made to bosses/subordinates are unreliably honoured. Strained relationships at the top damage relationships lower down. Essential cross-linkages between the functions may not take place, so that the functions become isolated from each other. That isolation leads to a loss of added value. Managers lower down do not recognise the contribution other functions could make. Furthermore, they do not appreciate the problems and concerns of other functions. When, inevitably, something does go wrong on the few cross-linkages that do occur, one manager blames the other as inadequate or even as causing an unnecessary and burdensome cost. Very quickly, a culture of poor communication, resentment, defensiveness and low trust spreads throughout the organisation.

Thereby, a split senior team inevitably affects employee morale. A telling statement to have emerged from the survey, 'Senior executives could be more tolerant of each other', was made in organisations where chairmen/CEOs, directors and GMs rated the organisation as facing difficulties, and the top team as not providing cohesive and consistent leadership. The lack of consistency of behaviour at the top, and lack of coherence of communication from the top, leaves staff and lower-level management feeling isolated and negative towards the organisation. The feeling that the changes that have taken place are misguided was consistently reported in organisations exhibiting these symptoms. Furthermore, the fundamental systems, disciplines and administration required for the effective functioning of the organisation are identified as a hindrance and bureaucratic. In effect, the key organisational processes, traditions and identity of the company are not respected.

At a personal level, what initially emerges as a loss of challenge and drop in job satisfaction, if allowed to fester turns into resentment and finally a loss of confidence, whereby not only the individual, but also his home life is adversely influenced. The tensions and dissatisfactions of work are taken home, upsetting family relationships.

Once the morale of management begins to slide, so, too, does the morale of employees, but for the latter that slide is more difficult to control and reverse.

In certain exceptional cases, the senior management may sincerely hold different, well-thought through views on the future of the organisation, but the negative effects outlined are not visible. The reason is that the senior team members are disciplined. There exists a fundamental respect for the views of colleagues and a recognition that to mismanage the process of negotiating the future of the company would seriously damage the fabric of the organisation. In the survey, one organisation was identified in which two of the directors, with the full support of their colleagues, resigned and were considerably assisted to find alternative employment. The reason for the resignations was that the two directors strongly held different views from the others concerning the future direction and shape of the organisation. However, the process of managing out those differences was one based on respect; respect for others holding different views; respect for the stability and integrity of the management of the organisation.

Differences of vision can be competently addressed, in a way in which neither individuals, the team, the organisation, its employees nor the infrastructure is damaged. In most cases, however, differences of vision induce conflicts, painful resignations, opportunity costs and lost business. If the members of the top team pull in different directions, harm occurs. Differences of view go hand in hand with poor judgement and a mismanagement of the processes of negotiating out differences in order to form a strong and cohesive team. Knowing where you are going and knowing how to manage getting there are integrally combined elements of vision.

Managing differences of opinion is one problem. Unfortunately, another is that certain top managers are simply unable to cope with the process of identifying and implementing vision. There are executives who are *vision vulnerable*.

VISION VULNERABILITY

Certain senior managers are unable to appreciate the processes and steps needed to establish a realistic and pragmatic way forward that would enhance the business. Three reasons have been identified: not seeing the wood for the trees; being in transition; and not knowing what the figures mean.

Not seeing the wood for the trees

A person's ability to identify, work with and organise the level of detail required, effectively and in an operational sense, to manage the business, may not be matched by the ability to extrapolate from that detail a sufficiently clear view of the shape and direction of the business for the future. Such a person's judgement is clouded by too much detail; in effect, he is unable to stand back from short-term concerns, which are necessary for decisions on operational matters, but which are, as a result of the volume of information, a drawback to formulating strategies for the future.

This person is too preoccupied with short-term concerns and is thereby not capable of debating and identifying longer-term issues.

41

Typically, such a person has been employed in the organisation for a considerable period. He has offered good service in the past and is probably respected and reasonably well known. He has been promoted to general management as much because of good service in the past, as because he has displayed the potential for senior office. Alternatively, he may not have worked in the company for long, but is reasonably well known in the industry and has a sound track record.

Once into general management, the destructive impact of a wrong appointment for both the appointee and the organisation is soon felt. The immediate subordinates of the appointee, from their hands-on experience of the company, know only too well when inappropriate or poorly thought-through views about the future are being expressed. Those same subordinates also recognise when their boss cannot coherently project a view about the future. Initially, subordinates may respond sympathetically, but such sentiments quickly turn to resentment, as the guidance which they need in order to provide identity and meaning to their roles is not forthcoming.

For the appointee, the inability to provide a coherent view of the shape and direction that the business should pursue can prove to be distressing. Subordinates are unlikely to tell their boss that he is not performing, but he feels their resentment. Furthermore, as the appointee is more comfortable with detail, he is likely to be overinvolved with the work of his subordinates. The boss wants 'to check out what's happening'. In response, they may resist such close attention, which is viewed as interference and distrust.

Giving feedback to your boss to the effect that he is not providing the necessary guidance and direction is such a delicate process that most subordinates would not do so. If some attempt to offer feedback indicating that a more strategic orientation is required, the conversation could easily become too general and ephemeral. For the senior manager grounded in detail, that is further confirmation that strategic discussion means wasting time.

Appointing effective middle managers to senior roles largely because of their previous management track record is a common practice. Some such appointments are successful. However, once an error of judgement is realised, there is little point in hoping that a wrongly appointed executive can find a way out of that situation. For the appointee and subordinates involved, the situation is too threatening to address effectively. In the short term, other senior managers may need to intervene to guide the appointee or help him leave. In the long term, an examination of the assessment and promotion process is required.

Being in transition

How long does it take for a newly appointed senior managers to successfully negotiate their learning curve and emerge as effective as the first day he was appointed? In exceptional cases, up to 60 months from the date of appointment; on average, however, 20–30 months. Another group of vision-vulnerable managers are either those newly appointed to a role of general management, or those with experience of general management who have been promoted or changed companies.

It is recognised that employees enter into a learning curve each time they change jobs. The way the learning experience is managed considerably influences the long-term contribution of the appointee. To move on too quickly, simply because the newly appointed person is confronted with problems, may mean that the appointee does not gain sufficient experience and hence does not fully mature into a position of command. The lack of maturity shows in the next appointment. To stay and negotiate the job change in a poorly managed situation can be a damaging experience for the appointee and his subordinates. Hence, understanding the learning curve is crucial to the future successful performance of the executive.

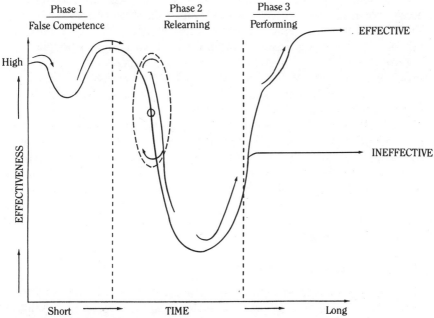

Figure 1.1 *The transition curve*

The original and interesting Parker and Lewis (1980) study outlined the stages of learning and experiences of people who undergo job change, captured in what they termed the transition curve. Broadly, three phases of transition are identified (Figure 1.1).

Phase 1: false competence

A person has been promoted to a general management position. Whether the appointment is internal or external, it is highly likely that the person has been appointed because he is considered effective. On starting the new job, work effectiveness inevitably drops. The surroundings are new, work issues may be difficult to understand, and, because of the range of tasks to undertake, the job may seem overwhelming. Especially for a manager newly appointed to general management, simply coming to terms with how to relate to other senior executives may naturally induce reticence. The way things are done is sufficiently unfamiliar to the appointee that he feels unable to make plans or even to function adequately.

In the vast majority of cases, the appointee within a matter of weeks or months, becomes accustomed to the demands of the new role. He develops the confidence to make a contribution in meetings. He sufficiently breaks down barriers between himself and senior colleagues to discuss shared concerns or pressures. Advice and sympathy may be offered by others as to how to go about handling particular issues or people.

Within a relatively short period, the initial experience of reticence, shock and even immobilisation has subsided. The appointee is likely to consider himself to have emerged from the learning curve and to be beginning to operate effectively. Having broken down barriers between himself and the other members of the senior group so as to converse sensibly, and having become accustomed to the initial demands of the job, the appointee naturally feels he is ready to accept full responsibility.

At this stage, however, the appointee is more than likely drawing upon the skills and drives utilised in the last job! In essence, he has entered the stage of false competence – the honeymoon period – the belief that the skills, knowledge and experiences developed in the last job can be applied to the present role.

Phase 2: relearning

From the immobilisation and false glamour of phase 1, the appointee enters into the relearning stage when he begins to recognise that the demands made by others cannot be met by simply using old skills and experiences. Phase 1 provided the time for temporary retreat as the appointee reoriented himself to the new job and organisation. However, within a reasonable period of time, others cease to treat him as a new appointee. They want him to become part of the team. For the appointee, the realities of the change now become obvious – he faces the strain of performing as is really required by the situation! That's the central issue, for what does learning to be effective mean under particular circumstances?

If he is newly appointed to general management, coming to terms with the considerably greater discretion in role is crucial. Forming a view as to the shape and direction of the function/unit for which he is accountable is important. The process of convincing colleagues of the strategies to pursue is equally important, as colleagues need to trust the judgement and capacity of the appointee. Hence, thinking about what one needs to do, not arguing on behalf of hastily formed views concerning strategies and objectives, has to be coupled with having the confidence to manage and nurture relationships and crucial interfaces with the key personalities at that senior level.

For the appointee who already has experience of general management, relearning largely involves coming to terms with the *true* meaning of effectiveness in the new job. Recognising the role challenges and constraints facing the appointee is the first step. The questions to be asked are the following:

- To what extent are the accountabilities and responsibilities in the new role well aligned?

- To what extent am I being held to account for undertakings for which I am or am not responsible?

- To what extent am I, as the senior manager, attempting to control my situation by adopting a dictatorial style with my immediate subordinates, reducing their role to virtually that of clerks? – or making far better use of them by patiently building up a relationship of trust?

In the short term, the dictatorial style works. People do what is required of them but little more. From the strategic-thinking and forging-ahead point of view, it does not work, for the team concept becomes redundant. Furthermore, what is likely to happen to a senior manager who may conclude that the accountabilities and responsibilities in his new role are not well aligned? In effect, he is held accountable for activities for which he is not responsible. Under such circumstances, feelings of threat, anxiety, insecurity and lack of confidence may pervade the judgement and personal will of the senior manager, so that what is learnt is skill at deflecting accountabilities – more commonly known as 'passing the buck'. If relearning is learning how to pass the buck, the appointee, the team and the organisation suffer.

Recognising what the other key people are like, and how to nurture relationships with them, is a crucial second step. The questions relevant here are the following:

- What are the attitudes of the members of the top team?

- To what extent are there positive and enabling or undermining and disabling relationships and behaviours exhibited among the members of the top team?

- To what extent is it important to nurture particular relationships with influential figures in the senior group – who are the culture makers?

Learning how to interact with the new subordinates, colleagues or bosses in a manner that is sufficiently comfortable to them is crucial. Teams and organisations have their own particular identity, their norms of thinking and behaving. Learning to become part of the group, managing key relationships well, and consciously attempting to integrate oneself into the senior group are necessary if the appointee is to make an impact.

The new appointee in general management has to become accustomed not only to the personalities and relationships but also to the decision-making processes, the degree of exposure in role, and, most of all, to methods of vision formation for the future. The learning is greater and deeper. The new appointee has to undergo considerable relearning in terms of understanding how to fit into these new circumstances. He has to come to terms with what effectiveness really means, to discover what are the sensitive issues that need tact, timing and consideration in order for them to be meaningfully addressed, and to what extent do issues of ego and personality pervade discussions of business and strategy.

With such a considerable relearning to be worked through, it is easy to see how errors can occur.

Case Study 1.5

YOU'VE GOT TO HANDLE US DIFFERENTLY

Edward Kingsley, a former SAS major, had seen action in the various troubled parts of the world, including Northern Ireland. Physically fit, professional in combat, softly spoken, one of the genuinely few officers who are as respected by their superiors as trusted by the officers and soldiers under their command, he retired from the armed forces.

With his experiences, demeanour, and alertness and the graduate qualification he obtained studying part-time in the army, he was soon offered employment. He accepted a middle-management position with a large brewery company. Within two years, he had quickly risen through the 'ranks' and had been appointed general manager of the West Region, namely Somerset, Devon and Cornwall.

The West Region had been a problem – sales were down and falling – for the third year in succession. The outgoing GM had stated that the region was too prone to the cyclical ups and downs of the tourist trade. Edward, within the first few weeks of his appointment, found a poor regional team that clearly had lost touch with its key clients – not the public, but the publicans. So not knowing whether the problem was the tourist trade or a poor regional team of functional managers, Edward did what he always did as an officer – if you want to know what it feels like to be a foot soldier, go and do it yourself.

So he did just that – he had a few drinks in a few of his own pubs. He discovered just how out of touch was his regional team with the publicans – certain pubs were renovated, they should never have been; other pubs with a potentially extensive and upper-income client base were losing business to competitors because both the premises and the publicans were shabby. Edward, with his regional team, set about generating meaningful marketing plans, setting realistic sales objectives, targeting particular pubs for refurbishment, as they were classified *high net-worth revenue sources*, held meetings, and made presentations to the publicans on future developments. The strategy worked – loss of sales was stemmed, revenue grew considerably, and the cyclical tourist trade turned out to be less of an influence on sales than was first expected. Trade was as much won by enticing local customers away from competitor outlets, as by attracting more tourists.

Edward's bosses had marked his progress with interest. It was common knowledge that the MD, Leisure Division, was to retire within the next 2–3 years, with Edward being the favourite up-and-coming candidate for the job. In order to prove his value, Edward was given one more region – Scotland.

Within a few weeks of his new appointment, Edward faced the same sort of situation as before, a poor regional team of functional managers, not appreciating what sales and marketing meant for them and seemingly out of touch with the needs of the publicans. What to do? – same as before – walk the streets and have a drink.

However, this time, events did not turn out as well. With much the same openness and friendliness of style, Edward made himself known to the publicans, to be greeted on a number of occasions with what seemed to be suspicion. Edward continued with his visits to meet greater suspicion, which even extended to his own regional managers in Edinburgh.

One particularly frustrating day, Edward's secretary had been trying to organise a meeting between him and his regional managers to find that one or more of the individuals was not available on any of the dates given. Edward sent a memo – a three-line whip – telling his regional managers to turn up on a particular date at a particular time. A few days later, Edward's MD rang him from London.

'Why are you saying you are going to sack the Scottish regional managers?'

'What?' exclaimed Edward. He then heard an astounding tale that the regional managers had rung their dotted-line bosses at headquarters in London, indicating they had received a memo stating they were about to be fired.

Although Edward pacified his boss, his relationship with his immediate subordinates and his overall standing in the Scottish community worsened, much in line with his ever-diminishing sales revenue for the region.

Within nine months, Edward was transferred to a far smaller region, where he is now beginning to make a positive impact.

Just before he left Edinburgh, two of his team made the effort to say goodbye to him. With one, the finance manager, Edward had had a better relationship than with the others. The two slowly entered into a conversation as to what had gone right and wrong with Edward's stewardship of the Scottish region. At the end of the conversation, the finance manager remarked,

'Edward, I understand more now, but we're not the same people as in Devon. You've got to handle us differently. This is a close-knit community.'

It took Edward some time to come to terms with where he went wrong. After all, getting to know the people had worked in the past.

Once in the learning curve, mistiming statements and actions, mismanaging important relationships, not knowing what questions to ask because the appointee has not bothered or not known how to go about appreciating the true nature of the situation he faces, are common occurrences. As an officer, Edward, in Case Study 1.5, was known by his subordinates. He was in an authority structure in which command and compliance go hand in hand. In the West Country, Edward was like a breath of fresh air, genuinely enquiring about the state of the business among well-established and transient communities. In Scotland, in well-established communities and with Edward's reputation preceding him, genuine enquiry was interpreted as snooping; receiving memos was interpreted as being one step away from being fired! In Scotland, Edward moved too fast, he thought that others, like him, were concerned only with business results. He failed to recognise that spending time to nurture relationships was a vital first step to gaining results. For Edward, nurturing relationships meant exuding charm, not devoting time to getting to know, getting to understand and ensuring ownership. Simply, Edward did not recognise that business is done differently in Scotland.

Anxiety and even depression and loss of confidence are commonly reported experiences during phase 2. For many, that depression is a first step to relearning. The appointee is facing the fact that he has to change. What worked in the past will not necessarily work here, as performance is deteriorating and something has to be done. Edward has both learned from and matured during his Scottish experience.

Others resist learning and enter into the 'O' factor, going round and round in circles, becoming frustrated and depressed, and then blaming others and convincing themselves that others have the problem, not them. Depending on the culture of the organisation and the nature of the markets, individuals can stay in their 'O' factor for years, reducing the performance of others around them to a considerable extent.

Phase 3: becoming effective

By letting go of past behaviours, attitudes and expectations, and trying to develop new competencies suitable for the new job, the appointee is attempting to work his way through his transition by accepting a new reality, a new challenge. He is likely to become more proactive. He may try out new behaviours, new work styles and new approaches, and apply newly learned skills. This testing stage is as frustrating as the second stage. The appointee is bound to make mistakes, become angry with himself and irritable with others. These negative feelings have to be coped with. He attempts to put his new world together, through the application of styles appropriate to the situation. He seeks for new meaning as to how and why things are now different.

Becoming accustomed to the new responsibilities, thinking through what direction and identity to provide in the new role, and learning not to accept the status quo but to test and practise new philosophies, attitudes and behaviours are common experiences during phase 3. In addition to testing, phase 3 involves a process of internalisation, whereby new philosophies, attitudes and behaviours are adopted, together with what is left of the old attitudes and behaviours. The appointee has consolidated his thinking, direction and position, and, with new confidence, is now operating at a higher rate of effectiveness than the day he was appointed.

It is at this stage that the appointee clearly begins to recognise the nature of the markets in which the company operates, the need to maintain positive relationships with suppliers, distributors and other support services, and the true preparedness of the organisation to function. It is at this stage that workable strategies for shaping the future begin to emerge, with realistic attempts to implement them, first through having them accepted by the members of the top team, and then passing them down the organisation.

Experience has shown that the more senior the appointment, the greater the likely depth and width of curve, the greater the need for effectively managing people, adopting appropriate attitudes, and making the time for communicating adequately. No matter how insightful the emerging vision, if the appointee has not been able to fit in well with bosses and peers, then it is unlikely that these people will trust him or his capability for high office. Certainly, whether newly appointed to general management or with experience of general management, each person who changes jobs will experience, to a greater or lesser degree, the transition curve. Some, through experience, learn to manage change, so that the trough of the transition will not be too deep nor the length of time too great. Others do not seem to learn from past experience.

An *ineffectively* negotiated transition occurs when an appointee has made inaccurate assumptions about the business, and/or has ineffectively negotiated the necessary quality of relationships required to run the business. Unless there is a chance of improving the situation, it is time to leave.

Throughout the whole transition phase, the appointee should attempt to develop a high quality of relationship with bosses and peers, so that, whatever is said or intended to be done, others trust him. As a result, they will feel responsible for what he feels is necessary to do. Similarly, they will excuse mistakes that are made.

Not knowing what the figures mean

Because of either being in transition,

or

not knowing the differences for his business between sales and marketing,

or

not knowing the level of costs required to stimulate appropriate revenue streams,

or

not having the skill or conviction to tell corporate bosses that they have not fully appreciated the nature of the business,

the head of a business unit may end up not knowing *what the figures mean*.

Knowing what the figures mean refers to a senior manager being able realistically to appreciate market circumstances and the capacity of the organisation to pursue particular objectives, from the analysis of statistical data, such as sales forecasts.

When the head of a business enterprise, or key function, requests information from subordinates which indicates the projected performance of the organisation over the short to medium term, but can neither accept the data he is given, nor trust the ability of subordinates to produce accurate forecasts, then he is in danger of not knowing what the figures mean. The subordinates state that they have accurately assessed current market trends and the likely revenues to be attained. The boss might view the forecasts as too conservative and consider increased perform-ance feasible. At the time, it is difficult to ascertain who has miscalculated the situation, the boss or the subordinates. With time, it becomes obvious which of the two parties really appreciated what the projected figures represented in terms of attainable business goals.

Case Study 1.6

FRANK SAYS, 'DO IT AGAIN'

'Frank says, do it again – you must have got it wrong. We're targeted for 22 per cent revenue growth!'

Peter Rice, European president of a North American hi-tech company, had just fin-ished briefing his top team, the European functional vice presidents and country GMs. They had presented to him their sales and costs forecasts for the next half-year. Essentially, costs were predicted to rise 5 per cent while revenues were predicted to grow 14 per cent from last year's performance.

'There's no point in doing that,' commented the director of sales. 'I've been through all the figures and worked with the country GMs. Fourteen per cent across the board is ambitious. I doubt whether Spain and Benelux are going to hit their targets as contribution to the 14 per cent.

Peter Rice was not interested.

'You guys have got to get your people to rework the figures. I don't care how you do it – cut costs or increase revenue – we need more from you sales guys – just do it!'

Susan Chamberlain, European group Human Resources director, said, quietly,

'I think to send the figures back down for them to be reworked is a waste of time. The figures do nothing more than realistically represent what we can do! Alterna-tively, to cut costs is likely to damage the fabric of the business – we will cut costs to a point where we cannot trade any more. It's not worth our telling our people to rework the figures as a paper exercise when it's going to make no difference to our year-end results. What's more, reworking the figures is likely to demotivate our people. They will know they are just playing games with numbers.'

Peter just looked at her. The others knew that the relationship between Peter and her had long been frosty. They could not see Susan surviving in the organisation much longer.

'I don't think the figures are the problem, Peter. I think you should tell us what you are going to do to help us sort out Frank,' stated Susan.

'What do you mean?'

'The figures are real. It's Frank who does not understand the European business. That's been the case for some time, even before you came. He's been changing the figures round and then accusing us of getting our forecasts wrong and of not

---

knowing our business, and that's not true. We just don't know how to handle Frank. You know him, you've worked with him, you even joined the corporation within two years of each other. What are you going to do to change this around, Peter?' enquired Susan.

Peter Rice looked at her again.

'Before I came here, I looked at the European business and I gave my word to Frank that it was realistic that by my second year, revenue would be increased by over 20 per cent,' stated Peter, quietly but very firmly.

'How the hell can you run a European business at arm's length from the States? Just because you promised Frank, even before you were placed on an expat contract . . .'

Susan's voice trailed off. She knew she had said too much. Peter icily remarked,

'Not all expats just want to go home clean, pleasing their corporate bosses. Some of us do care about our placements.'

Silence.

'I don't think there is more to say. We need to rework the figures to have them ready for the next board meeting, which is where? – OK, yes, Milan. That's up to you to organise, Frederico [Italian GM]. OK?'

The group nodded. Susan said nothing. She did not stay for the drinks and socialising after the meeting.

Peter Rice (Case Study 1.6) did not survive long as European president. The end-of-year performance indicated an increase in sales of 12.5 per cent. Frank stated that Peter had misled the corporate board by making predictions of 20–22 per cent increase. When Peter protested that he had been browbeaten into making such forecasts, Frank accused him of dishonesty.

'If there's one thing I need from my regional presidents, it's for them to tell me the truth.'

Shortly after that, Peter resigned, but in the meantime so had Susan Chamberlain – and the sales VP and the manufacturing VP. The European structure was disbanded, the remaining team members were turned into a management committee, reporting to a North American president in Ottawa. This year's forecasts indicate a drop in sales. The North American president is planning, with the European committee, a strategy for cutting costs.

The reason that mid-to-large-sized corporations and especially multinationals seem particularly prone to misreading market trends and to forecasting poorly is that the top managers have not taken the time to appreciate what sales and marketing really means in the different regions of the world. The limited-tenure appointment of most expatriate contracts, aggravates the situation by introducing an unnecessary level of short termism.

Most vulnerable are those executives well steeped in the tradition and culture of the coporation. They are likely to have intimate knowledge of the products/services produced by the company, and an accurate understanding of sales and marketing within their home market. However, having spent too long in the home market makes them vulnerable to failure to recognise that other parts of the world are not the same. The products may need customising, and the processes of sales and marketing are different, and, hence, establishing a presence in new markets may take longer than expected.

An emerging meaningful phrase is *globalisation*', highlighting the need to think realistically about how to create an effective worldwide business. The case study analyses repeatedly displayed the difficult problems faced by US corporations in conducting business in Europe as part of a globalisation strategy. Coming to terms with the facts that Europe is not one market, but many, and that quarterly financial reporting is an alien concept to many Europeans, has not been an easy process for certain US corporations.

The checklist below identifies the key influences on growth, in terms of increasing market share.

What key influences lead to increasing market share?

- Top management: all top-team members need to display positive attitudes to growth.

- Mission: needs to be clearly communicated.

- Corporate centre: offers support for the operating businesses.

- Management style: top team adopts a management style of valuing the performance of others.

Fundamentally, the top management is the prime influence for effectively or ineffectively expanding the organisation. The attitudes and styles adopted, the ability to communicate, and the capacity to operate in markets shared with equally competitive and quality-oriented competitors are essential. Globalisation is not just a problem of size. Globalisation, or the ability to manage on a grand scale internationally, is a 'people' challenge in terms of recognising different cultural conditions and responding with appropriate styles and behaviours to suit the new organisational structures. Globalisation is as much an interface problem between corporate headquarters and regional subsidiaries as it is an economic issue of growth. If top management does not understand, not develop and not recruit appropriate local management, problems arise, namely those of not supporting relevant market strategies, not appreciating regional consumer and competitor behaviour, not making appropriate investment, and, hence, not generating desired profitability.

Lack of sensitivity to learning to operate in unfamiliar markets, not taking the time to appreciate the sales and marketing processes in new product or regional territories, and insufficient guidance on expatriate placement are likely to generate another problem, namely, not being able to tell the difference between personnel and structure problems. Is the prime reason for failure the senior manager in post, or the result of trying to work a poorly configured structure?

Peter Rice's departure (Case Study 1.6), accompanied by a disbandment of the European structure, indicated corporate headquarters' need to control future developments so as not to repeat the problems of the past. However, whether the new structure is conducive to expanding a European business is in question. In reality, the corporate headquarters' executive exhibited little understanding of the nature of the problems of its European subsidiary – was Peter Rice placed in an impossible situation or was the real problem Peter Rice himself, his relationship with his own subordinates, and his relationship with corporate headquarters?

The costs of not knowing whether the organisation faces personnel or structure problems can be substantial. Apart from the immediate costs of reorganisation and relocation of executives, the opportunity costs of lost business and poorly exploited business opportunities can be immeasurable.

BEST PRACTICE INVENTORY

Dos

- [ ] Once in a senior management role, consider what *managing discretion* really means in the new role. Managing discretion involves making choices as to what can be achieved and how objectives are to be achieved.

- [ ] Become intimately acquainted with the challenges and problems facing the function or organisation for which you are accountable. Realistically recognising what objectives to pursue or how to achieve them depends on having formed a sufficiently detailed understanding of the present circumstances of the organisation. Insist on being briefed. Talk to the right people.

- [ ] Come to terms with the fact that generating a vision for the future will have long-term viability only if it is shared by the members of the executive.

☐ As a part of the sharing process, create a sufficiently open atmosphere in order to discuss strategic options, differing views as to sales and marketing, the relationship between the operating businesses and corporate centre, and, most important, the commitment each senior manager in the team feels towards these issues. Not until each key manager indicates what he really thinks and feels about the issues in question, will there be any sense of shared commitment to move forward.

☐ Be prepared to overcome resistance, blockage, splits and personal animosity within the top team as well as the overall executive. Generating a shared view for the future is as much the result of opening up a dialogue for logical debate as it is of dealing with people's emotions. It is important to have considered how to handle both.

☐ Recognise that splits of vision within the top team may require the departure of one or more members of the group. The manner in which any senior manager departs is of crucial concern, for the team members will need to feel a confidence in each other in order to work together. Reallocating the membership of the team needs sensitive management in order to ensure a viable group identity for the future.

Don'ts

☐ Once in a new job, do not declare your position on key issues prematurely. Recognise what really needs to be learnt in the new situation and also the amount of time you need to emerge successfully from the learning curve.

☐ Do not assume that because a particular style, approach or strategy worked in the past, it will work in the new circumstances. Whatever worked in the past may or may not work currently. It is vital to examine present circumstances in order to appreciate what are feasible ways forward.

☐ Do not commit yourself to achieving ambitious targets if you are not intimately acquainted with the circumstances surrounding the new posting. If, unfortunately, such strong expectations cannot be initially renegotiated, then, at least, ensure that vital channels of communication are kept open between yourself and other key top managers. You may be placed in a situation of having to re-educate your bosses as to what it is feasible to achieve within particular time frames. Nurture that communication channel and do not hide from the responsibility of using it!

As can be seen, much depends on the attitudes and behaviours of the members of the top team. Key business conversations can be encouraged or discouraged according to the shared understanding and commitment to the vision and strategies identified. Thinking about the business and managing people go hand in hand.

Shaping the team is critical in shaping the future.

2

Shaping the Team

Q: *What importance do you attribute to good teamwork at the top?*

A: Oh, essential! I mean the most important thing in business . . .
Any endeavour which requires more than one person to do it,
must have a team spirit. A team requires individuals, all of
whom have a quality that is unique to them compared to others
and respected by others.

Gordon Owen,
Group Managing Director, Cable and Wireless,
Chairman, Mercury Communications Ltd

Especially in central London, Mercury Communications is visible – in
the rather impressive, variously coloured phones – which are not British
Telecom phones. Mercury, however, is far more than just a few phones.
Mercury is big business, thanks to Gordon Owen. Initiated in September
1984, with Gordon trying to spend £1 billion and expanding to 7000 people,
Mercury achieved profitability within five years, profits that are in nine-
figure numbers. Mercury's turnover, currently, is over £800 million.

Gordon Owen has an impressive track record of success, which he
attributes mostly to effective teamwork.

TEAM MECHANICS

Teams are necessary for the continued growth, development and daily
management of a business. Yet, in how many teams have members experienced positive, forward-looking, fruitful, added-value experiences,
whereby, even if the work load may be immense, the professional pride
and personal satisfaction from being a member of that team is a significant and memorable experience in one's working life? The survey
response is 'uncomfortably few'.

■ Seventy-six per cent of GMs feel negative about their immediate
bosses in the senior team.

■ Fifty-two per cent of chairmen, CEOs, MDs feel uncomfortable about the effectiveness of the senior team and the performance of its members.

■ Fifty-six per cent of CEOs, MDs and GMs, feel there are important sensitive issues at top level which remain unaddressed.

■ Sixty-six per cent of senior managers recognise that substantial hindrances obstruct the senior team in achieving objectives.

In the survey, this question was asked of top management: 'If matters do not improve in the top team, will the business be affected?' The answer given is yes, the business will be affected. In particular, management and employees would be affected in terms of morale and drive to perform well. The members of the top team would be affected in terms of deteriorating relationships, and, by implication, the future of the company would be affected.

Our experience as researchers and consultants strongly suggests that teams are vital; they are not a luxury, but a necessity for the effective functioning of the organisation. The reason teams are so important at senior-management levels is that they are the prime mechanism for the consideration and implementation of policies and strategies! Senior managers need a forum where they can discuss the fundamental issues that face the organisation, and identify and agree to implement approaches that will address current and future concerns and challenges.

Manufacturing cannot produce products of which sales and marketing have absolutely no knowledge or experience. Some consideration, however crude, will have taken place so as to co-ordinate the production with the market exploitation of products. Finance and human resources need to interact with the other functions simply to justify their existence. It would be difficult to obtain and understand figures representing commercial performance without the finance function interrelating with the line functions. It is impossible to recruit, develop, pay and make people redundant, if the human-resource function does not co-ordinate with the line functions.

In effect, senior executives work in groups. Top UK managers were asked: How much better would the company be if the top team performed better and resolved key issues? The responses indicate that matters would dramatically improve. In particular, strategic and personnel issues, such as sales and marketing, employee morale, internal relations and overall performance from employees, could be better managed. Interestingly, improving internal relations and stimulating greater performance from employees were rated as high as improving sales and marketing. The personnel and business issues are integrally combined.

In the short to medium term, individuals and organisations can *muddle through*, considerably dependent on the professionalism, will and endeavour of supervisors and middle managers. In certain organisations, it is surprising just how long, short to medium term really is, as the pride, expertise and standards of quality of the lower and middle ranks of management keep the place going.

However, time does catch up and does catch one out. The people and strategic issues insidiously present themselves as operational problems in terms of staff turnover, low morale, loss of market share, increasing costs and poor product/service quality. What seemed like an irritant yesterday can become an inability to induce added value today.

What is a team?

A team is both a forum for discussion, decision making, and identifying strategies for policy/operational implementation, and an environment – an ambience – which enables or disables the processes of discussion, decision making, and implementation.

If the members of the top management group feel that the quality of relationships, the openness of discussion, the commitment to the decisions reached, and the discipline to implement the decisions made are good, they would probably call their group a *team* – a stimulating, positive, enabling forum within which to maintain a dialogue. If the members of the top management group identify the relationships, decision making and implementation processes as tolerable, but need to create a degree of formality and structure in order to ensure that the agenda is addressed, that group may be called by its members a *committee*. If the members of the top management group consider the quality of their relationship to be negative, and the decision making to be poor, with little commitment to implementation, the group may be seen as 'those so-and-sos that I have to work with on a regular basis' – at best, just a forum where certain meetings take place.

Poor-quality relationships need not exist. To create an effective team at the top is entirely in the hands of the members of the top management of the organisation. Shaping a disparate group of executives into a more cohesive team involves consideration of six factors:

1. Key forum for dialogue.
2. Reacting to each other.
3. Respect.
4. Opportunity costs.
5. The way you say it.
6. Styles and philosophy of management.

The key forum for dialogue

For a director of finance, what is the most important part of the job – the finance part or the director part? For a director with regional/countrywide responsibilities, what is the most important part of the job – the regional part or the director part? Observation indicates that the senior manager himself determines which part of his job, the functional/regional part or the corporate director part, gains prominence. Whichever part is more dominant, the other is not eliminated; it is just not as important.

The director part of the job is the representative/corporate identity part, whereby the senior manager represents the issues of the function and the likely contribution the function can make to the corporate whole. It is not the senior manager's prerogative to state what his function will or will not contribute to the body corporate, for that is the result of discussion among the members of the top team. What role and contribution the personnel function should play depends as much on the needs and views of the other directors, as on the aspirations of the personnel director.

Even the functional elements of the job are not totally within the senior manager's control. He may present the performance of the function/region for which he is responsible and project the likely performance in the future. Colleagues may require a different level of performance to suit the circumstances of the overall organisation. He may disagree, and even resist the views of colleagues, but is likely eventually to take account of those views. The personnel director, for example, may recommend the most ideal system of conducting appraisals, only to be told that line management is unable or unwilling to adopt the best practice, leaving the personnel director little option but to introduce a system that line management desires, but which he knows is not the best available.

Therefore, whether the senior manager prefers to emphasise the functional parts of the job or the corporate director part, he cannot ignore the fact that the director part of the job involves his representing issues for debate with colleagues who have the right to support or contradict what he is doing in his job.

Once in the corporate team, no man is an island.

Reacting to each other

As each senior manager represents the issues of his function/region/product area, indicates the expected level of performance over the next period, and highlights how his function is to relate to the larger corporate organisation, the members of the group are considerably exposed to each other. A member's view of his function; his view of the contribution of the function to the overall organisation; his view of the shape, size, out-look and image of the overall organisation; and his personality and style; all these become enmeshed. What one has to say and the particulars of his personality influence the perception of others. In high office, per-sonal characteristics stand out to a point where it is difficult to deter-mine whether a person himself or the strength of his argument is the dominant influence on others. Accompanying such exposure is the need for emotional resilience to sustain performance in high office. Being continually exposed to comment, criticism and the demands of others can, for some, be an overwhelming experience. After a while, they simply cannot cope. Hence, a flexible mind and personal strength go hand in hand as requirements for effective performance in high office.

Respect

A fundamental requirement for effective performance in the senior exec-utive group is *respect*. If the members of the senior team do not respect one another as people, as professional managers and as decision makers, the relationships between the individuals deteriorate rapidly. Lack of respect is synonymous with lack of trust. Lack of trust among colleagues can lead to conflict, confrontation, divisiveness, defensiveness in the sense of protecting one's own area of responsibility, and, certainly, a block to group progress towards corporate objectives.

Opportunity costs

Lack of respect and lack of trust lead to a deterioration of relationships among the members of the senior team. Living and working under such circumstances is personally unpleasant and damaging to the business. Because the relationships are not sufficiently robust, people talk to each other less about key issues. While it is all too easy to address simple con-cerns or offer good news, it is taxing to discuss sensitive concerns and complex problems. A confidence and openness of style are required if, as a part of a strategic debate, you need to express to a colleague that you are dissatisfied with his performance.

After a while, senior managers who do not talk sufficiently to each other are likely to be unaware of developments in the market, or of internal problems until such problems become obvious. In effect, opportunity costs are likely to arise if poor executive relationships are allowed to fester (see Chapter 6, for an analysis of the impact of opportunity costs on the business). What at first may seem to be an irritant could over a period

61

become a major problem. Becoming accustomed to living in a situation of opportunity costs makes people less sensitive to the need for quick and positive response to problems, so that, after a while, corporate life seems to lurch from crisis to crisis.

The way you say it

Executive relationships rarely deteriorate rapidly and dramatically. Irritation and frustration, sometimes leading to more open conflict, take time to develop over a number of meetings and interactions and over a number of issues.

Teams that are well able to address sensitive and non-sensitive operational and strategic issues evolve a pattern of interaction which is sufficiently comfortable to enable each of the team members to discuss issues, as well as talk about personalities. That does not mean that the team members do not experience discomfort. Controlled discussion as well as confrontation can take place, but in a manner that is acceptable to the group. Essentially, the relationships between the members of the group have been sufficiently well nurtured, so that each member can offer views and give feedback where necessary.

In less effective teams, tensions are quickly felt. Members guard what they say. In extreme situations, members are conscious that they may be misinterpreted, so that even the most innocent of issues which could be perceived as threatening are not debated. Issues remain unresolved, negatively affecting the organisation. In such an environment, relationships have not been nurtured. Any form of on-the-job team building is unlikely to have taken place.

Styles and philosophy of management

Gradually, senior managers do evolve a style and a philosophy of management. The two in combination provide for the more fundamental views each executive holds concerning how the organisation should be managed, how people should be handled, and with which other managers each easily identifies. The style or styles and philosophy of management indicate the depth of feeling as to how people wish to be managed and spoken to, or how they should interact with others – I am open; I want others to be open, to speak their minds, to be team players, to be individualists and entrepreneurs. For others, communication is not so important. For yet others, discipline in terms of identifying with the policies and procedures of the company is their deeply held philosophy.

The quality of interaction between the members of the senior group is crucially influenced by the mix and match of the style or styles and philosophy of the members of the senior team. The skill is to manage the people in the senior team in a manner that is both conducive to focusing each person's attention on the key issues, and nurturing in each a sense of commitment and ownership towards the organisation. Managing people effectively, handling different personalities, addressing their beliefs and values in a way acceptable to them, while still keeping them, as people, focused on the business, is a process fraught with pitfalls.

In the study of US CEOs conducted by Charles Margerison and myself, it was no surprise to identify the key stressor at work as managing people – especially one's own immediate subordinates (see Appendix B). The strains and stresses of juggling with sensitive but crucial relationships do come home to roost. Managers need to be adequately prepared for the process of managing people, relationship building, and ensuring commitment to implementation.

SHAPING THE PEOPLE; SHAPING THE TEAM

Partly because of the exposure that accompanies appointment to senior office – so much attention is on senior managers that others can see what they are really like – and partly because of the potentially intense nature of working within the senior team, group members rapidly become acquainted with each other. The range of personalities, as well as the business challenges facing the organisation, influences the range, type and quality of conversations in the team.

In my experience as a consultant and researcher, most executives are more than sufficiently capable of recognising the nature of the problems they and their organisation face. All of the executives I encountered, understood and had formed views as to the nature of their work-oriented problems. Not all within the same team had formed similar conclusions. Some may have understood their problems, but were unclear as to how to proceed. Some were unwilling to disclose what they really felt and thought about their circumstances, needing to feel confidence in me before they discussed their situation more openly. All, however, basically knew what was happening to them.

Many consultants present to clients, verbally or in reports, what the client already knows. Certain clients may feel comfort that someone else has recognised their problems – a problem shared is a problem halved. Other clients, however, express irritation that they are being told something they already know – surely, they should be getting more for their money! We concluded that with most senior managers, there is little to be gained by offering insights into the nature of that organisation's problems.

Hence, if insight is not the problem, what is?

The problem is 'actioning insight!' – using the insights that one already has to overcome the feeling that one cannot do much about the problems one knows one has! Not only do managers recognise the nature of their problems, but they also learn to live with them because of the feeling that they can do little to change the situation. Even when the levels of personal discomfort become high, they prefer to live with their problems although they and their situation deteriorate, and business performance dips.

At director level, continuous discomfort is synonymous with poor executive relationships. Handling the personalities in the group may be perceived as so strenuous, that key conversations do not take place where they should – in the boardroom or the executive committee. Instead, conversations about how to tackle the problems being faced take place at private dinner parties, over a drink, or even at casual meetings in corridors, but rarely at the constituted meeting.

Senior managers in trouble need help to put into action the already rich insights they hold as to how they could move forward, by examining the way they conduct their affairs.

The quality of interaction among the members of the senior executive can enhance or damage the business.

All the experts an organisation ever needs to address or solve its fundamental problems are in place, namely in the executive committee, or in the boardroom or wherever the top team meets. However, the manner in which the relationships have evolved could prevent the group members from utilising their expertise.

Key determinants of the quality of executive relationships are the style or styles and philosophy held by each member of that executive. If the underlying views and attitudes held are conducive to in-depth discussion about the business, its problems and its progress, then such discussion will take place. If the views and philosophy held by the group members negate satisfactory business conversations, then issues are likely to remain unaddressed and to fester. The ability to manage the people in a way that is acceptable to them but also conducive to business is a rare and highly valued skill.

The difference between an effective and ineffective team is not that a fundamental compatibility exists between the members, but that serious consideration has been given as to how the personalities in the senior team interrelate. In an effective team, attempts have been made to create an environment conducive to meaningful discussion about the business. This may involve inducing a certain amount of tension in the group, but not to the level of being debilitating.

Those senior managers who do not seriously consider the impact of the interrelationships of the personalities on the top team are not likely to have thought about the impact they personally make on the group in terms of stimulating positive relationships or in creating an open culture capable of inducing relevant and forthright conversation. Those who have considered their impact on their team colleagues, who have made attempts seriously to adjust their approach, and who have developed both a style and a philosophy conducive to the team and the business have *thought* about what they are doing. Those who have not thought about what they are doing have tended merely to *react* to their colleagues on the team.

STYLES OF MANAGEMENT

Six distinct styles and philosophies of management emerged from the research data. Two, the integrator and the discipline-oriented manager, are placed under the *thinker* category, and four under the *reactor* category.

The thinkers

Integrator oriented

The capacity simultaneously to recognise the problems, needs and challenges facing people within the organisation, coupled with a sensitivity to the demands of the market, are fundamental virtues of the integrator. The integrator tries to match the needs of the business, the levels of capacity and maturity of senior management, and the demands of the marketplace. As one highly successful executive indicated, 'I see the business through the eyes of my direct reports.'

The integrator makes the time to learn about the business. He has learnt how to withstand external pressure to act (and can control the temptation to respond), until he has reached a balanced view. The integrator is likely to spend time walking the floor, getting to know the problems and issues facing his immediate subordinates. He appreciates what the processes of sales and marketing mean for the business, whether converging or divergent views exist on how to improve performance in the marketplace, and what are the implications for the business if such convergence or divergence of view is allowed to continue. Essentially, the integrator becomes intimately acquainted with the details of the business, the people running the business, and developments in the marketplace.

Such a drive to learn emanates from an understanding that *ownership*

65

of the strategies being pursued and *identity* with the organisation are crucial. Without ownership and identity, nothing meaningful is likely to happen. Ownership of the policies and of the strategies being pursued must exist within the senior team. If senior managers do not identify with what they have decided, what hope is there of anything being effectively implemented? Once the top team members have truly appreciated the nature of the problems and challenges they face and the actions and practices required to improve, then it is possible to stimulate a shared commitment to progress. The approach of the integrator is to invest time and effort to stimulate a climate of commitment and, if necessary, hold back from implementing important decisions until such commitment is apparent.

Obtaining agreement, however, does not mean gaining commitment. Gaining commitment involves feeling confident that colleagues, bosses and subordinates are truly going to act upon what has been decided; in fact, it means observing both *coherence* and *consistency*. *Coherence* means being able to express clearly the concepts, issues and strategies to be pursued. If managers cannot talk about the issues at hand or express what they think or feel, they may not understand the issues in question or feel too uncomfortable or too threatened to express what they believe. *Consistency* refers to the actual behaviours exhibited in implementing strategies or decisions. If the members of the senior team do not carry out what they have agreed; if policies and strategies are inconsistently implemented across the function and department, the behaviour of those managers indicates a lack of ownership. The acid test is always, will people do what they say?

To ensure that issues of coherence and consistency are fully addressed, the integrator attempts to create an environment where full and open discussion of individuals and business issues can occur. The integrator will have recognised that debate about issues is insufficient. Discussing issues and giving feedback to individuals on their behaviour and comments have to go hand in hand in order to overcome barriers and generate the necessary levels of commitment.

In order to offer feedback with the intention that that feedback be sincerely considered, the integrator needs to show that he can receive and well handle feedback by having *nurtured relationships* within the top team in order to create a level of *comfort* for focused and intense business conversation to take place. Relationships need to be sufficiently robust in order that a healthy feedback process should take place. Feedback is not just expressing one's views and feelings clearly. Feedback also means 'building up' other people to receive the message. (See Chapter 5 for an analysis of feedback.)

Case Study 2.1

TOP COP

A newly appointed chief constable quickly discovered that his senior team members were too rule-bound, were out of touch with the problems of their junior officers and constables, but, most of all, were not talking to each other about the key issues facing policing in that police force. With the added strain of a hostile press, a suspicious local council, and a less than sympathetic Home Office, something needed to be done.

One afternoon, in spring, the chief called to his office his immediate team to announce that they should cancel all Friday morning appointments for the rest of the year. They were to spend that time with him, all Friday morning, drinking coffee and talking to each other on first-name terms.

The bewilderment of the deputy and assistant chiefs was natural but what could they do? – they had to turn up. That first morning, the coffee was good, but the conversation stilted. The problem was what to talk about!

The range of topics covered that morning was impressive, from the rise of Liverpool FC and the unpredictable performance of Manchester United, to gardening and the memorable occasion that Gary Sobers hit six sixes in one over. The silences in between became too uncomfortable and the only way out was – drink coffee. By lunchtime, at least two of the party were near to becoming health-drink fanatics. The chief, however, was the perfect host. He took part in the conversations, rarely contradicted his team, smiled, and drank more coffee than the rest. At 12.30 pm he invited his team to lunch; two accepted.

Next week, by Thursday, the tension was mounting – the problem was that tomorrow was Friday.

For the second Friday meeting, the coffee again was good, the chief smiled, and the conversation was more stilted than before, the reason being that last week, time could be filled by talking about the history of football. This week, there was only one week's worth of football to talk about with the inevitable result that the silences were longer and more coffee was drunk. The impact of drinking coffee had reached the point of pain – it just hurt to drink more.

The most extroverted assistant chief constable in the group, turned to his chief and said,

'What the bloody hell are we doing here, sir?'

The chief, smiling as ever, looked at him and said,

'Well, it's exactly the same as what you've been doing in your job for the last 16 years – bloody nothing!'

The group stared at the chief; the message was clear – talk seriously about the business of policing or drink coffee until Christmas.

Within three months, not only had the group begun to rethink the policies and strategies of that force, but they had agreed to transfer personnel from one department to another and were now talking about effective budget forecasting and budget management – unheard of before.

The chief knew why he had gone through this charade. The lack of ownership of strategy, the inconsistency of behaviour among the members of the senior management team, had left top management with little respect in the eyes of the rest of the force. Improving the standing of the top team would improve morale.

The chief, however, had another reason. He not only wanted to improve morale; he also wanted to delegate greater financial and managerial discretion to the inspectors – the first real managerial rung of the executive. How could the problems and disaffection within the community be addressed, if the rank of inspector was not empowered to respond positively to community problems. If, however, the inspectors were not supported by the superintendents and chief superintendents, what could the inspectors do?

Who could push a strategy of delegation down the line? – the top team could. Hence, the coffee management technique – a technique that is forceful, but not aggressive, and one which certainly induced ownership.

In Case Study 2.1, the plan of providing for the inspectors' greater freedom for community affairs through increasing their responsibilities and accountabilities could have been jeopardised by the lack of maturity of senior and middle management, namely the chief inspectors, superintendents and chief superintendents. Attitudes had been allowed to stagnate until the arrival of the new chief. The first step to change was meaningfully to address the attitude problem in the top team, so that an effective, step-by-step-change programme could be introduced, supported by the senior management group.

In my conversation with the chief constable in the early days of his appointment, I asked how long it would take to introduce change so that an observable difference of performance occurred at inspector level. He predicted 36 months from the date of his appointment. He was out by one month. In the 37th month of his appointment, the job description and budget responsibilities of the inspector rank changed.

The capacity to see what is required and then pragmatically to 'work out' what to do, especially in terms of predicting time, underlies the qualities of the integrator-oriented executive. The need for flexibility is paramount. In certain circumstances, he may have to adopt a softer, supportive, comfort-oriented style with colleagues and immediate subordinates because of the low levels of morale in the organisation – people need building up. Alternatively, the senior team could be too comfortable to appreciate, or respond to, demands from the market. In response, a tension-oriented style may be necessary in order to remove the lethargy.

The integrator recognises that the manner in which issues are addressed – the process – is as important as the issues to be addressed.

Impact on others
The recognition of what can practically be achieved and the patience to work step-by-step towards attainable objectives rubs off on others. The reason the integrator can recognise the reality of a situation and what to do is that he has learnt *maturity* (see Chapter 5). The integrator has learnt to distance his own emotion from the situation in order to examine what are appropriate ways forward. Such maturity is infectious. By learning to talk to one another and by fully addressing concerns, top managers become issues-based. Trust of each other, ownership of the issues, and commitment to effective implementation of decisions become normal – in fact, in highly effective organisations, so normal that these senior managers are surprised to discover the nature of problems in other organisations. Soon these senior managers behave like their bosses – as integrators.

Impact on the organisation
Once the integrator has positively influenced his team, that impact is likely to pervade the organisation, creating a culture of maturity and a positive orientation to performance. The predominant style is one of *openness* coupled with a sense of quiet discipline, where people count.

> Q: *Are there any sensitivities within the top executive that you could identify in terms of issues that need to be discussed, but are not discussed?*
>
> A: I cannot think of any. There were issues in the past, I think as much chemistry as substantial issues. I would say that the way we want to run our business and issues that confront us in the business, of who your enemies are and of how we can increase our market share, how we can launch new products, how we can make acquisitions, is almost friction free – pretty unusual.

Dr Tony O'Reilly,
President, Chairman, CEO,
HJ Heinz Co

The talented and tireless Tony O'Reilly has an impressive track record of, currently, £6 billion sales worldwide, profits of £500 million after tax, a return on equity of 26½ per cent, a return on invested capital of 30 per cent, manufacturing facilities in 19 countries, and a marketing presence in 152 countries. He comments, 'Most importantly, we have taken our margins from 30 per cent gross margins to 40 per cent gross margins in the last 10 years.' Tony O'Reilly recognises what it takes to integrate a structure of 45,000 employees to attain such business results. The key is good teamwork at the top, as well as no turf wars, an extensive ownership of the stock, through stock options, and an ability to read situations and utilise personality and style to positive effect.

Within such a positive culture, an accurate sense of realism pervades the organisation. Commitments made are commitments honoured. The business culture is one where the products and services are of the right quality and delivered on time.

Discipline-oriented

Discipline-oriented managers hold a high respect for the structure of the organisation, for the formal relationships within the structure, and for efficient application of the administration, systems and procedures. In effect, the senior manager identifies with the current establishment and strives to improve the efficiency of the administration. At times accused of being bureaucratic because of the identity with the administrative status quo, such managers have recognised that a well-run, disciplined organisation is fundamental to success. Consequently, it is important for them and others to follow established but meaningful work procedures. In so doing, discipline-oriented individuals pay attention to details and demand that others do likewise. They desire that others be well disciplined also, and, as a result, they respect people who 'stick to the rules'.

By exhibiting personal discipline and attention to detail, such a manager is more likely to ensure that decisions made and agreements reached are implemented and tracked in order to ensure efficient application.

Impact on others

By paying attention to details and establishing a discipline of following procedures, such managers are likely to be respected for their thoroughness and efficiency. It is unlikely, however, that they would exude an attractive style unless they particularly concentrate on improving their styles of managing people and projecting a positive image.

The discipline-oriented manager needs to pay particular attention to style, for, although his outlook of efficiency would be recognised, his personal impact on other key managers in the structure could be demotivating. What for him may be discipline and efficiency, others could perceive as inflexibility. By being too systems-oriented, he may appear to be insensitive to the problems of particular divisions, units, or departments, and he may be accused of being unable to adjust to local conditions. Furthermore, if he is not sensitive as to how his personal style affects colleagues, others may not even wish to enter into conversation with him, feeling that they would be wasting time or even over-exposing themselves. However, attention to improving personal relations overcomes such difficulties.

Impact on organisation
Discipline-oriented managers are likely to establish a culture of attention to detail and thoroughness, especially on issues of costs and expenditure. If coupled with a sensitivity to market/customer conditions and to staff and management, he is likely to be seen running a tight ship.

> The fundamental good running of the business is maintained in the disciplines of the company; without that no other decisions work, so there's no substitute for seeing that you have a well-disciplined and soundly based reporting business that is only involved where it should be involved. My best example of that is if you take the whole capital expenditure process, in our case we reckoned that having agreed our budgets, we'd turn round capital expenditure decisions within 48 hours, except on difficult major issues. In the area of people ... I would expect to always see, frequently for ten minutes, no more, the next level, apart from those you personally appoint. This gives you a sense of depth in the business, and also gives those joining the business a sense of accessibility to the centre of the business.
>
> Michael Pickard,
> Chief Executive, Sears plc

Interestingly, the need for efficiency coupled with good people management is highlighted.

To judge Michael Pickard's success, one need only look at how he, together with his chairman, Geoffrey Maitland Smith, has directed Sears' interests in retail and property. Names such as Saxone, Dolcis, Freeman Hardy and Willis, Freeman (the mail-order group), Selfridges, Fosters, Hornes, Adams, Olympus, Millets, Miss Selfridge, and Mappin and Webb are household names, and they are still only part of the Sears Group.

Senior managers who hold discipline-oriented values can be most effective if they realise that their natural attributes of efficiency and attention to detail need to be coupled with an understanding of market circumstances, and the personal impact they make on the organisation. Furthermore, they need to establish a culture of effective internal and external communication, attributes which are not natural for that type of person. Once discipline-oriented managers recognise that they themselves need to develop in the job, they are likely to emerge as high-calibre top managers.

Reactors

Self-made syndrome

Managers who behave as self-made, value *independence* – they feel they need to manage relationships, undertake and manage work activities, and make decisions, their way. The need for considerable personal space and for the expression of their own views and needs, are predominant concerns. Perceived encroachment upon their personal space is viewed negatively. Suggestions and ideas which seem to contradict their ideas and inputs which are seen to interrupt their flow of thought are perceived as irritants which may need to be removed. Only compliance with their own ideas is viewed as positive.

The reason such managers have evolved this self-oriented approach is that they feel themselves to be self-made. Typical is the owner/manager entrepreneur whose drive, ideas and charm with customers/clients, suppliers, distributors, and financiers, ie crucial external contacts, established the business and made it successful. However, he has not adjusted to running a more sophisticated and larger organisation. He has still to appreciate that he does not always have to emerge with the 'right' ideas; he does not need to be the only driving force in the organisation.

In practice, the term *delegation* is not understood by such a manager. The concept of team is interpreted more as an extention of himself, his ideas and ego, than as a mechanism for attending to the needs of a more complex structure operating, probably, in a number of markets. He has not learnt that the self-made way of the past is no longer relevant – in fact, is now a disadvantage.

Impact on others
Being at the receiving end of this independence-oriented approach is likely to be an uncomfortable experience. Knowing what to say, or even how to say it, is a problem. Despite the accuracy of the insights of the members of the team concerning developments in the marketplace, or the internal preparedness (or lack of it) of the organisation to address external issues or challenges, a level of anxiety can quickly emerge among the team members as to how to communicate with such a manager. In fact, meaningful communication may or may not take place. Time and again in the case studies, I observed members of top teams who had long recognised the nature of their problems, but felt such discomfort that they could not communicate their concerns, especially with a strong, unapproachable boss. Because of the level of discomfort, the situation in an organisation could deteriorate appreciably before any action is taken. When action is finally taken, it is often dramatic. The members of a board

voting their founder/chairman off the board is not uncommon.

Even as a subordinate, the self-made manager could have stimulated such discomfort among colleagues and bosses that they, finding themselves unable to confront him, do nothing. Sometimes, they hope that the situation may improve, but find little or no progress in terms of improving executive relationships or discussion of sensitive issues. Dismissing the manager in question and consequently being vulnerable to litigation for unfair or constructive dismissal is a situation which frequently occurs. In such a case, the delicate situation exposed in public could tarnish the image of the company.

Surprisingly, the manager concerned may not be aware of the resentment he is generating, or if he is, then he fails to recognise the negative business impact of such resentment. He sees it as trying to create an effective business organisation against all odds. For him, the incompetence, slowness and lack of insight of others are the problems. Hence his need to be even more forceful. As others do not meaningfully talk to him, he remains even more convinced that the problem is others and not himself. In the words of one vice-president of marketing, located in corporate headquarters in a US hi-tech company and seen to be badly mismanaging his dotted-line relationship with his regional marketing managers, 'I know it's them that are the problem, because if it was me they would tell me!'

This person's lack of skill led to the organisation's losing sales and not sufficiently penetrating its existing customer bases, let alone considering how to attack new ones. His strong personality and abrasiveness of style made it difficult for even the CEO to address him, with the end result that, after considerable pain and tension, he was dismissed.

Impact on the organisation
Despite the vice-president of marketing's departure, certain problems remained. Even up to general management level, the regions mistrusted corporate headquarters because of its insensitivity towards them and for having allowed the situation to so deteriorate before acting. Today, in the eyes of the regional GMs, corporate headquarters is uncaring, indecisive and too concerned with its own levels of personal comfort to care about the business. Considerable time and attention now need to be given to repairing a series of damaged but important relationships, at a time when all effort needs to be focused on sales.

Hence, the impact of too dominant a personality could not only split the senior team and divorce corporate headquarters from the rest of the business, but also, even after he has gone, leave a role model of inappropriate executive behaviour. That model is, get your own way, take little notice of others, only aggression works. Others are there to do only what

73

you tell them. Once a sufficient number of managers identify with such sentiments, then a culture – an accepted way of doing things – becomes established, and a management style of being self-oriented is interwoven into the fabric of the organisation. Once a sufficient number of managers identify with such a style, the organisation depends largely on the energy and drive of particular executives. Being systematic and organised is seen as something close to bureaucracy. In effect, the organisation becomes short-term-sales oriented. The level of teamwork necessary for the pursuit of long-term strategy, for the effective implementation of decisions, and for generating a business philosophy suitable for the organisation, is unlikely to emerge, or even be recognised as a need.

As we scan the financial pages of the more serious daily and Sunday newspapers, examples repeatedly emerge of overdominant senior managers who have been voted off the board, leaving behind a trail of tarnished relationships and organisations at risk. The retail trade has had more than its fair share of such experiences. Similarly, the financial-services sector has also made the headlines. Such organisation problems are likely to have been well appreciated within the company for some time, and the fact that little has been done to redress the situation is entirely due to the interplay of personalities in the senior group. The opportunity costs facing such an organisation are potentially high.

Only-what-they-need-to-know oriented

Managers who communicate with others on an *only what they need to know basis* have evolved a style and philosophy of *low disclosure* – they describe little about how they think and feel, and communicate the minimum necessary for others to complete tasks. This more closed or limited communication style is unlikely to arise simply because of a lack of skill to communicate or interact with people. It is more than likely to arise because communication is not recognised as necessary. A strong underlying sentiment could be that subordinates should do just what is required of them. People and the organisation are viewed as parts of a system which simply needs instruction in order for it to perform.

Why?

The manager concerned may have become used to doing tasks on his own, either because of his specialism or because of his inability to delegate. As a specialist, there may have been little requirement for him to delegate. In the past, he may not have had the trained staff available to form a team. Whatever the reasons, the manager has become used to working on his own, an attribute which emerges as an inability to communicate once he is appointed to general management.

Alternatively, he has not appreciated the processes of developing others to be sufficiently capable and mature to accept delegation. His experience has been that he achieves more on his own than with others. Checking out plans or ideas is viewed as slowing things down rather than adding anything of value. His experience indicates that the mistakes of others can be avoided if he undertakes to complete the tasks himself.

The reason such sentiments emerge is that the manager possibly still holds a task orientation – he simply wants to get jobs done, and few can do them as fast or as well as he. He has not matured into high office and has not appreciated that implementing policies and strategies is done through others. He has not appreciated that communication does not just involve clearly telling others what to do, and that he needs to spend time in nurturing relationships so that others feel comfortable with their boss and can discuss and question what he wants, in order to implement effectively what is required of them. Without that feeling of comfort, subordinates are unlikely to enter into a dialogue as to the most appropriate ways of achieving objectives or meeting the boss's requirements.

Impact on others
The immediate impact on colleagues or subordinates is that they are unlikely to understand the nature of the relationship between them and the uncommunicative manager. They are unlikely to understand whether they have done a good or a bad job. Without basic feedback, subordinates tend to do only the minimum necessary, partly because they are unclear as to what else is required, and partly because of their own anxieties about scapegoating. They have learnt that *to think too much means getting it wrong* – which the boss does not like! Hence, no real application is given to problem solving or innovative rethinking of issues.

Strategic issues can be reduced to the status of operational tasks. Senior managers can be reduced to the status of office boys – doing only what they are told.

Case Study 2.2

BRUNO LE CLERC

The president of a European motor manufacturer appointed Bruno Le Clerc, a Frenchman, GM, UK. Bruno's track record in the corporation was impressive, having held appointments in both line and support functions, as well as corporate headquarters. From the very start, the relationship between the British senior functional managers and Bruno was strained. Bruno made no attempt to visit his

---

colleague executives in their part of the organisation. Even today, five years after his appointment, Bruno has not visited all of the key regional sales offices, only the ones within easy reach of his office. Bruno held one-to-one meetings with the key managers asking them to account for the levels of cost and expenditure.

The British managers took exception to his behaviour, but what could they do? With no explanation, Bruno issued memos requesting information, and held most meetings on a one-to-one basis.

Attention to control of costs, however, did not increase revenue. The problem faced by the organisation was a classic one of sales and marketing. The division of duties between the two functions was unclear; duplication of roles and resources between the two had existed for some time; communication between the directors of sales and marketing had for a time been non-existent, a pattern of behaviour adopted by the sales and marketing personnel lower down the hierarchy. The principal clients – the dealers – had learnt how to use this disarrayed organisation to their advantage. If they could not negotiate the agreement they desired with their main contact person, they would link with other people they knew in the organisation to see if they could negotiate an agreement more in their favour. In effect, the dealers played one part of the business against the other. The sales strategy of penetrating client organisations through different people in order to gain access to key people and make a favourable sale was now being used by the clients on the company. Hence, not only were sales down, but also price differentials existed on the same product, or even product line, according to who was involved in making the sale.

Bruno's policy of cost containment and control has dramatically cut expenditure. The organisation now looks healthier. But as there is insufficient discussion about market conditions, there seems to be little or no shared understanding in the senior team as to whether the cut backs have begun to bite into the fabric of the organisation to the point that they have damaged its ability to trade. Certainly, morale in the organisation is low. There is no particular impetus to address external market conditions. Staff and management have learnt to respond rapidly to Bruno's requests for figures – they give him more figures but what do they mean?

In Case Study 2.2, Bruno does not communicate, but is disciplined in ensuring adherence to relevant internal procedures and administration. Making sure the system works need not be demotivating. Not communicating and not spending time with people can considerably reduce morale. Certainly, Bruno has not been able to induce added-value performance from his people. He has not learnt that by not communicating with his staff, by not raising morale, he is losing money. He has not recognised that the motivation of staff and increasing revenue are integrally linked.

Impact on the organisation
Poor or non-existent communication and the feelings of anxiety that can emanate from persistent low levels of disclosure are likely to become norms in the organisation. Managers do not consider it relevant to practise

communication – they just want others to do what they are told. Relatively quickly, a culture of defensiveness and resentment emerges and takes a grip on the organisation. The defensiveness arises from fear of making mistakes. The old hands in the organisation advise the younger ones to do just what they have to and no more, it is not worth it! People learn not to think.

The resentment arises from being treated, or the feeling of being treated, in a negative manner. Mistakes and problems are highlighted. Good work and effective performance are barely praised or not mentioned at all. Worst of all, scapegoating, or the fear of it, leads to an underlying dislike of senior management. Within such an environment, to expect any identity or ownership of the strategies and policies proposed by top management is unrealistic. Even positively minded middle-level managers are likely to become disillusioned and fail to practise fundamental disciplines, such as follow-through, leaving subordinates with the impression that even good management has given up.

With the wrong sort of leadership in place, performance can diminish rapidly, leaving the organisation in a constant state of poor morale. In effect, the future survival of the business depends on the continued professionalism of middle- and lower-level management and staff, and on stability in the marketplace.

The over-sensitive oriented manager

Certain senior managers seem to display considerable sensitivity as to how they are, and should be, approached. At times, they appear to be quite emotional, allowing their mood to influence their judgement of people and situations. They judge others by their manner, their overall conduct, and whether they seem to be on the same wavelength as the senior manager in question. They favour bosses, colleagues and subordinates who seem optimistic and pleasant, but others that seem cold and distant they may view as unacceptable. If people are judged by what they seem and not by what they do, such judgement may be clouded. They judge others simply on the nature of their interactions. Interactions that are perceived as supportive are viewed positively and could be the real reason for rewarding or agreeing with the supportive person's policies and strategies. People whose behaviours or interactions are perceived to be inappropriate or even distasteful are likely to have their proposals rejected, disregarded, or put to one side.

Ironically, the over-sensitive manager may see himself as being effective at managing people, highlighting his capacity to relate to others and be supportive when it counts. He thinks it positive that he is guided by his feelings about others and may openly claim to use his heart as much as his head when deciding what to do next. Undoubtedly, such sensitivities are a virtue. To know how to handle others, relate to them, and recognise before others the problems that are likely to arise with particular individuals are positive features.

However, what distinguishes a sensitive person from one who is *over-sensitive* is that the over-sensitive person is likely to take criticism personally, no matter what the intention of the other party making the comments. It is the person's over-sensitivity to how others feel about him that influences his behaviour. By being so emotional, the manager's appreciation of the contribution of his colleagues and subordinates, or of the pressures and problems colleagues and subordinates face in their roles, may be considerably clouded. It may be difficult for the over-sensitive manager to distinguish between the role demands, challenges, constraints and functional requirements facing colleagues and subordinates in their jobs, and the personal performance of any one manager.

Managers who find themselves in a difficult situation for business reasons, or because they are over-exposed in a poorly configured structure, may be accused of poor performance simply because their behaviour irritates or threatens the over-sensitive senior manager. The over-sensitive manager would give little thought as to why such a manager is behaving poorly or underperforming. The manager is simply disliked.

Hence, for the over-sensitive senior manager, one response is to blame others. Another is to blame himself. The over-sensitive manager may see the problems of the organisation, or the poor performance of others, as his fault. He overestimates the degree to which he should be held responsible for problems that arise. Whether he blames others or blames himself, such emotions not only cloud the professional judgement of the senior manager, but affect his level of energy and contribution. After a while, he simply feels drained, stressed or even depressed, and performs below par.

Impact on others

The charm, emotionality and, at times, erratic behaviour of the over-sensitive individual is likely to leave others with different impressions – some singing his praises and others expressing alarm or antipathy. Those who can get on with him are likely to feel motivated as fully contributing members of a team. Others are likely to dislike the way they are treated. Certainly, very few feel neutral about such a person.

As far as clients are concerned, the mercurial nature of the over-sensitive manager is likely to make him attractive. Because of his capacity for emotionality, he can relate well to people, especially on first meeting them, or at occasional meetings. Clients are likely to see him as charming, sensitive and responsive to their needs. Clients are likely to express considerable surprise on discovering that tensions exist within the top team or within the organisation.

Most people are likely to find such a manager a problem in his running of meetings. The manner in which he conducts meetings may be as much dictated by mood, as by the agenda items and issues at hand. Discussions could fly off in different directions. Sometimes, meetings may be long, yet fail to complete the items on the agenda. At other times, meetings may be short, to the point and comprehensive. Those out of favour may find it difficult to represent the issues of their function/ department because they are not heard. Those in favour would probably be able to address even sensitive issues, without fear of scapegoating. Certainly, one meeting is unlikely to be like another. Some will learn to live with and manage such a person. Others will find the strain of interacting with him unacceptable, and they will resign or attempt to remove him.

Impact on the organisation

The position held by the over-sensitive senior manager in the structure is crucial in terms of impact on the organisation. If he is a head of a function dependent on the performance and contribution of that function, he may either be tolerated or pushed to leave. If he is the CEO/MD of the organisation, then, in practice, the whole strategy of the organisation could be determined by the mood swings of that person. The organisation could be run according to the neurosis of one individual.

Case Study 2.3

THE MONEY MEN BEHIND THE SCENES

One fast-growing, eye-catching, and entrepreneurial finance house in the City of London is today facing problems.

Its CEO is an energetic, intellectually capable man who has little time for administration and people (although he denies the latter). Meetings are poorly run, with many of the relevant issues, in practice, being brought to the attention of the boss on a one-to-one basis. Those who have learnt to survive and function in the organisation, have learnt that managing the boss in a sensitive and personal way is important, as it is only then that he feels comfortable in discussing and addressing concerns. In meetings when the boss feels threatened or criticised, he blames the other party for not having presented well or handled the meeting well.

The mood swings of the boss generate considerable anxiety in a number of the members of the top team. The other senior managers do not know with what they are to be confronted from one day to the next. Those who have known the boss for some time feel there is not much of a problem – 'You simply have to get on the right side of him!'

Others perceive a considerable problem. They cannot trust decisions made in the top team, as decisions are changed after meetings. Nor do they know what the CEO is going to say in private or in public; whether he is going to embarrass them by saying or doing something that might undermine their role; or whether something going wrong in their area of responsibility is going to be highlighted.

Not surprisingly, middle managers have little trust and faith in senior management. Life to them seems like a series of crises, with little or no support emanating from the top. Most middle managers are tired of working in what they describe as a 'neurotic organisation'; they feel abused without being able to say why.

Because middle and senior managers have been appointed from the ranks and are, at heart, financiers, the problem is seen by some of the members of the top team as one of not having the necessary professional middle management to stabilise and expand a successful business.

There is some truth in that, but, in this case, the prescription of 'give them some management training' is not going to help. Sorting out the top is!

In Case Study 2.3, the inconsistency, unpredictability and the anxieties that are generated could lead the organisation to be in a permanent state of crisis management, lurching from one serious problem to the next. Because of not meaningfully addressing long-term issues, and the top team's not being consistent and disciplined in what it does, the organisation seems to be beset with problems – of its own making – an admission unlikely to emerge from the top. Just as in the case of the chief (Case Study 2.1), it's someone else's fault.

In contradiction to Tom Peters' message (in *Thriving on Chaos*) that innovation and development emerge from environments where there exists a certain degree of organisational chaos, research clearly shows that it does not! Peters, in attempting to capture the US business experience, seems not to have appreciated that in the best-run US companies, innovation emerges because of discipline, a clear understanding as to what to invest in and why, with people working towards clearly defined objectives in clearly defined jobs, in an environment where a basic sense of calm prevails. Exactly the same applies to the best-run UK and Irish companies. Certainly, innovative teams may seem chaotic because they are given considerable latitude to explore. Successful innovative teams, be they in R & D or sales, however, are disciplined, project oriented, goal focused, and really able to work only when stability is provided. Discipline and stability are the bedrock for the latitude necessary for innovation. Look at the Japanese; they literally have a mountain of wealth from appropriately and well-applied discipline and stability.

The Specialist orientated

Executives who value being specialists are those who identify with a particular profession, discipline or expertise. Those who are like them they understand. Communication is considerably easier among others who hold a similar professional orientation. Communication problems can arise with people who do not identify with, or understand, the values of that profession or that specialist manager. The reason for such an impediment is that the specialist has been over-exposed to very particular ways of thinking, a particular language and approach; that he is out of touch with the vagaries, ambiguities and blemishes of life. He has ceased thinking and communicating as a generalist. In the words of one CEO who wished to remain anonymous, 'Those guys that have spent all their life in one function have had their general management street skills kicked out of them.'

Such a person may have been too long in a particular specialist function such as finance, or a line function such as manufacturing. Hence, he finds it difficult to appreciate the overall general management implications of a situation and may not be able to appreciate the nature of the problems and sensitivities facing his colleagues. The specialist naturally sets high standards. His analysis of circumstances is likely to be accurate, but are his recommendations workable?

Not just in business but even in medicine one has to take the broader view. A recent article in the *Independent* (Monday, 5 March 1990) outlined the work of Dr Mary Hepburn, a consultant at the Glasgow Royal Maternity Hospital, who cares for pregnant drug addicts and prostitutes. Dr Hepburn's philosophy in helping others is to recognise how people actually live – 'It's no good telling patients what to do if their circumstances or beliefs make your solutions completely unrealistic.' That's a basic fact of life from which no one is exempt.

If one is to help and contribute, it must be done in relation to the circumstances of the situation. There is little point in the financial controller of a business forcefully arguing for greater cost control, to the point of demotivating the salesforce, when the business is facing a revenue problem. A balance between cutting costs and investing in people needs to be reached.

The single-minded focus, the high standards, and the, at times, critical approach of the specialist could leave colleagues cold. Even if the ideas are brilliant, the way they are sold could be off-putting and lead to the rejection of both the specialist and the recommendations made.

Impact on people

The immediate impact on others is that of someone who is insensitive to problems and circumstances outside his immediate experience. His narrowness of view and lack of basic understanding of how problems in different parts of the organisation arise, and whether certain problems are the result of poor management or of the nature of the function, may lead the specialist to inappropriately intervene with colleagues. Given the already vulnerable and exposed nature of any senior manager's role, for him to be confronted by a critical colleague who is not fully appreciative of the reasons for his problems, and who, from his point of view, is making inappropriate statements, can lead only to aggravation. Lack of appreciation of the problems of others not only leads to a rejection of the specialist's ideas, but can also place a strain on others as they are confronted with criticisms. Such strain leads to resentment.

Impact on the organisation

Once a senior manager becomes resented for his lack of sensitive or appropriate comments within the top team, not only he himself but also the function he represents may become isolated. Nobody wishes to use the services of the function, and, within a short period, the contribution (or lack of it) of the function is questioned. Traditionally, the finance and human-resources functions have been liable to be ignored, not respected, and even viewed as a 'necessary evil'.

'What the hell do personnel know about what we face in the line?' This is a comment I frequently heard in the survey. Numerous senior managers have emphasised how much people do not know, as their solution to most problems is another course or a new appraisal form. The contribution of the personnel function has been shown to be only patchily respected.

Another example coming to the fore over the last two decades of a function that has repeatedly been beset by problems of communication and isolation from the rest of the organisation, is information technology (IT) services. How to introduce IT to the rest of the organisation in a manner that has been of considerable concern. Especially with IT, the problem has been a human one – how can IT fit in with the rest of the business, not vice versa? For the head of IT, the answer, in principle, is simple. IT talks to its clients – namely the staff and management in the organisation.

Case Study 2.4

SIMON HUGHES

Simon Hughes is the head of IT in a large corporate bank. Simon grew up in IT. He served his apprenticeship as a computer programmer. From early on, he exhibited a flair for organisation and managing people, and relatively quickly progressed through the ranks to a fairly senior managerial position within IT, certainly senior enough to observe the impact of Fletcher Chambers, his boss and the then head of IT. Fletcher thought he knew the IT requirements of the rest of the bank. He certainly did not like the other GMs or regional executives criticising IT or even indicating that IT was not meeting the bank's needs.

When certain of the middle managers of the IT department in charge of teams working in the regions on the bank's IT problems indicated that the client had a point and that, really, a change of heart was required, Fletcher shouted at them and threw them out of his office. Certain of the more extrovert and devil-may-care middle managers shouted back and refused to get out of his office. Funnily enough, a number of them got their way.

For Simon, a far quieter and more gentle individual, Fletcher's approach seemed wrong. As the years went by, Simon became convinced that Fletcher's approach was destructive. Fletcher remained head of IT for eleven years. On his departure, Simon Hughes was promoted to the job.

Simon's approach was in complete contrast to that of his former boss. He quickly established liaison committees between IT and the rest of the bank in order to discuss, not only progress on projects, but also the range of IT needs of the bank, how to service such needs, staffing requirements, and complaints arising from within the bank on IT services. Simon has instructed his managers to recognise and refer to the rest of the bank as *clients*. Certain of his middle managers chair *client liaison groups* which discuss in detail particular problems on projects with a view to their satisfactory resolution as far as the client is concerned. All of Simon's middle and senior managers have been sent for management training, focusing especially on people management, client management and the marketing of professional services. Simon is generally acknowledged to have improved the position, status and service provided by IT.

However, he is still facing problems. Some say he is too soft. Others criticise him for being too lenient or too lax at meetings. One of his own middle managers recently commented,

'OK, they listen and make a big thing about listening, but they don't do much!'

His own staff and certain bankers have criticised Simon for being out of touch, because if he were more in touch, he would react sooner.

Simon is well aware of the criticisms. I recently sat down with him to discuss developments in his department.

'I know what people are saying, but how can I get rid of eleven years of misrule overnight?'

He stared at the wall behind my back.

'The clients want action because they think they know what they want. I know that on certain projects they do not, and if the project were allowed to progress, the objectives and actions agreed would have to change – that's expensive. What's more, certain of these clients would then blame us for not having guided them appropriately at the project-determination stage.'

'I see, but what about the reactions of your people?' I asked.

'Well, as you know, I have kept most of the old management who were under Fletcher, except one or two, in order to display support, cohesion and a new and positive identity for the future. They now want me to behave like Fletcher did. Tell the rest of the bloody bank what to do and where to get off! My people now say that Fletcher knew how to handle these flaming bankers and most of the time he was right. The reality was that Fletcher was right only some of the time – in fact, as far as I could see, only 50 per cent of the time.'

He stared back at the wall.

'I've just reached the most difficult phase of my stewardship. I've trained all the relevant managers both on the job and off the job, but now they have to mature. Our clients need to mature to be able to work with us. My people need to mature to be able to relate to clients who still require coaching and coaxing. I've simply got to do my best to bring my people on, meet more with the key clients, and, I hate to say it, survive.'

'I think you might be right, Simon,' I responded.

Those heads of support functions who have seen themselves as providing a necessary specialist internal service only according to what is best practice for that specialism have probably generated resentment and isolation of their function from the rest of the organisation. Those heads of support functions who have seen themselves as internal consultants, and who are attempting to understand the needs of the different parts of the business in order to gear their services to address those needs, are likely to be accepted by the rest of the organisation. However, as the Simon Hughes example highlights (Case Study 2.4 above), it is not always easy to change the attitude of a specialist to that of a mature, client-sensitive generalist.

Carol Ward, human resources director, Square D Corporation (Europe), says, 'I believe that it's important to operate in such a way that people trust you . . . There are some behaviours that do engender trust . . . It's coming back to people.' The reason Carol Ward is one of the up-and-coming executives of the 1990s is that she is not just effective as a head of human resources. She is also a competent strategist – she observes the problems and then attempts to place the human resources in line with corporate strategy.

The checklist below highlights the attitudes to emerge from top executives who hold a specialist orientation towards their job. Their emphasis is on promoting functional specialism. The behaviours required for strategic direction and communication are offered little respect.

Views of specialists on the top team:
Results from the survey

Statement

- More specialists are needed in positions of authority in this organisation.

- Work satisfaction comes from understanding the technical/ specialist side of my job.

- Members of the top team should identify more with the function/department rather than the body corporate.

Specialists appointed to general management positions but with little or no general management experience or training, are recognised as problematic. Too many specialists of a particular kind at the top can create fundamental strategic problems. UK manufacturing has long faced the problem of being product driven and not market led. Lack of understanding of the needs of customers and an overemphasis on the technicalities of the project easily occur when too many experts sit together at strategic decision-making levels.

In contrast, the ECC Group – English China Clay – a world leader in the field of industrial minerals, requires high levels of performance from senior managers both as specialists and general managers.

We see specialists as being important for the Group. If you have products which have world leadership behind them, technologically, you notably have specialists in the field. I don't think we find any problems in making overt distinctions between specialisms and general management . . . Indeed, many of the leaders of the ECC Group over the years have come from specialist groups . . . They have seen the relevance of internationalism . . . it is the ability of our people not so much to develop specialisms . . . but always to have a balanced approach. The most senior people are balanced people. We find they can mix specialisms with major roles as general managers, and this happens continuously throughout the Group.

Lord Henry Chilver,
Chairman,
ECC Group

Technological leader in R & D; dominant in the supply of kaolin; well integrated in terms of marketing, production, R & D, and extraction; strongly emphasising the need for, and practising, internal and external communication; ECC is effectively managing its business and addressing the issue of developing specialists to adapt to a general management view of the world. Not many companies have evolved such a positive ethos.

However, in many specialist operations, the specialists tend not to value business management skills. The meaning of terms such as sales and marketing, in practice, becomes confused. The skills of managing people are not given prominence. Making assumptions as to the degree of shared values and vision among the members of the top team is likely. The emphasis is on product and product technology instead of coupling such skills with those of branding. The emphasis is on specialist project teams, not pulling the people together to attack the market. One frustrated senior manager, in discussing with me how to change the nature and the culture of the top team in an attempt to stem diminishing revenues, said, 'It's simple – this place is run by our engineers and we all know what that means.'

BEST PRACTICE INVENTORY

Dos

- ☐ Understand yourself. Come to terms with what you are really like. Once appointed to a top job, your performance is as much influenced by the way you conceptualise as by your personality and style characteristics. In certain organisations and in certain circumstances, people are more concerned with what you are like rather than what you are.

- ☐ Understand the other key senior managers. Facilitating both a shared ownership of the issues to be addressed by the team and a commitment to act in a consistent manner requires managing the other key managers in a way adapted to the circumstances. Use any style that induces an outcome of shared ownership and commitment to act.

- ☐ Recognise that substantially different forces drive an organisation forward. If one were to draw a continuum identifying the prime motivators behind the key decisions made, at one end of the continuum would be logic and at the other end emotions.

Key influences on decision making

■————————————————————————————————■

Logic	Emotions
Business data	Personalities
Economic data	Mix of chemistry
Trends	Relationships
Extrapolation	

Decisions based on logic utilise data through identifying business and economic trends. From that data, and through a process of extrapolation, decisions are made. A decision-making process based on the interplay of personalities at the senior management levels is one that is driven by emotions. Who influences whom, who was the last one to see the boss after the meeting, and the overall mix of chemistries among personalities can all seriously influence the nature of the decisions made and their implementation. It is difficult to know what really drives an organisation, logical analysis or simply emotion and personalities. One will discover the reality of what goes on behind the scenes only once one is in the organisation.

☐ Take the time to reach a balanced view. Once into the job or the organisation, it takes time and sensitive investigation to form accurate conclusions as to what is happening and why. Forming a balanced view is the basis for putting into action the insights and expertise already in existence within the senior team. As indicated in this chapter, it is really astounding how many aware and competent people feel threatened, or are in the wrong job or organisation, or are blamed for events which are out of their control, and hence end up performing poorly. Not taking the time to reach a balanced view could mean underestimating the potential of your management.

Don'ts

☐ Do not assume too much too soon if the intention is to reach a balanced view.

No one person is the result of one experience or one characteristic. We are all a mixture. Close observation, however, suggests that one or a small number of dominant characteristics in a manager strongly influence his thinking, feelings and behaviour in role. The manner of behaviour, thinking and feeling, all of which are changeable if the manager recognises the need for change, strongly influence personal performance and the quality of interaction among senior colleagues.

The message is clear. People can change their style, philosophy and orientation. People can be trained, or managed, to change their style, philosophy and orientation. The first step is self-recognition as to one's own orientation and its impact on bosses, colleagues, subordinates and the overall organisation.

Shaping the team involves not only understanding and appropriately managing a potentially demanding group of people, but also recognising how the top team directly affects the overall business. Each of the members of the top team is likely to hold a crucial role in the structure of the organisation. The skill is to manage the people and the business at the same time.

By shaping the team, one is already *shaping the business*.

3
Shaping the Business

If you are not empowered to pursue your favoured marketing strategy,
why should you be responsible for performance targets?

Martin Sorrell,
CEO,
WPP Group plc
Speech to the Cranfield Management Association,
21 November 1989

People tend to produce profit-and-loss accounts at about a billion
pounds turnover level, and below that if you want profit centres you
need an army of accountants and transfer pricing, which is foolish.

Lord Tombs of Brailes,
Chairman,
Rolls Royce plc

Organisation structures are a means to an end. Structures are the means
by which resources and attention are focused to attain particular goals
and objectives. Resources can be allocated to people who are required to
discharge particular duties, and, who, in turn, are supervised and moni-
tored by others in the organisation. Organisation charts highlight how
the structure should operate, how work should be managed and the
manner in which key relationships are to be conducted. Organisation
charts identify the nature of the reporting relationship within and
between the levels of management, the nature of the relationship
between boards, committees and working groups, by exhibiting the
straight and dotted-line relationships that need to be respected and nurtured.

Martin Sorrell asks a common-sense question: if senior managers are
not given the latitude to do what they consider is best in the market,
how, then, is it reasonable to hold them accountable? Sorrell is referring
to the balance between accountabilities and responsibilities – a key concern in configuring an organisation structure. Lord Tombs highlights an
equally fundamental point, namely, what should be the shape and size of

the structure in order to induce the desired revenue streams, while at the same time maintaining effective cost management.

Structures, in addition to reporting relationships, identify job responsibilities and activities. Staff need some idea of what is expected of them in their jobs. The degree of definition of the task activities within any job and the degree of clarity of standards of performance required in that job influence the performance of staff. The size of the organisation; the formal relationships among staff; the formal relationships between functions and groups; and the clarity of the responsibilities, account-abilities and tasks attached to roles all strongly determine how staff and management within the structure are motivated to make the structure work.

Furthermore, structure is a powerful influence on culture. Anyone new to an organisation senses the shape, the dominant attitudes, and the underlying culture of any business. Walk into the reception area of a company and one immediately 'scents' the organisation. Is someone there to greet you, are you dealt with in a warm and polite way, can your requests be appropriately communicated to the relevant parties, are you kept waiting, do you have to walk for miles and go up and down in lifts to hold your meeting? The structure shapes the organisation. The people in the organisation then respond to that shape in their daily inter-actions, which eventually emerge as a distinct pattern of behaviour – the outward signs of the culture.

Shaping the business in a manner conducive to constant improve-ment of business performance is no easy task. The following questions are relevant:

- Is the present structure right – in fact, what is a right structure?

- Are the right people appointed to the key and sensitive roles that strongly influence the performance of the structure?

- Does the way the structure is configured induce the positive atti-tudes among staff and management necessary to stimulate constant improvements in performance?

- Is the manner in which the structure is administered appropriate to the needs of the organisation and its people?

THE SHAPE OF THE BUSINESS

In the survey, considerable differences of opinion were expressed by senior managers as to the range and type of organisation structures. In fact, within the same organisation differences of opinion were offered from senior management as to their current structural configuration. Prolonged observation, however, confirmed four basic structural types: functional, product, divisional, and matrix.

Functional structure

Functional structure involves grouping activities into departments or functions, each with a departmental or functional head, with the intention that all contribute to a common mission. The co-ordination of these departments is achieved through the appointment of an overall director, ie a managing director, supported by an executive committee or board. More of the companies surveyed (43 per cent) reported a functional structure than any other kind.

The advantage of the functional structure (Figure 3.1) is the simplicity of reporting relationships and co-ordination of activities, as well as the economies of scale in housing specialists within single departments from where they can be utilised across the organisation.

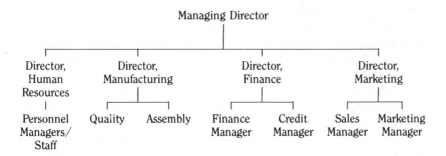

Figure 3.1 *Functional structure*

The disadvantage of the functional structure is the myopia that can arise because of the lack of liaison between the departments. True, specialist services may be housed under one roof ready for distribution according to need. Responsiveness to those needs is the issue. Recognising the nature of the problems of other departments, establishing a positive relationship with relevant departmental heads and other key staff, and acting to meet needs all depend considerably on the style and attitude of the key departmental heads in the structure. Considerable co-ordination skills are required in order to allow functional structures to work effectively. Only a limited number of the survey respondents indicated the importance of liaison in functional structures. Of those that did not, a substantial proportion reported destructive power plays between key managers in the organisation. An example of a high-performing, functionally structured organisation is the *Belfast Telegraph* (see Case Study 5.1). The openness by which key issues are addressed within the top team ensures the effective performance of this organisation. The leadership of Bob Crane has considerably contributed to the newspaper's continuing success. One notices, when meeting Bob and the team, the awareness the team members have for each other's issues and problems. They are well aware of what it would mean to slip into a more negative way of working and the ensuing co-ordination problems.

Product structure

Product structures (Figure 3.2) involve generating an infrastructure around particular product or service streams. Adopting a product structure is likely to involve a duplication of functional services, as each product or service stream is likely to have its own support mechanisms to service that stream. The advantage of such a structure is the emphasis given to product quality, in that sufficient attention can be given to the needs of each product or service range by attracting the necessary resources and qualified personnel to service that stream. The people who know most about the product are those who are promoted to managing the product streams. However, the survey identified particular difficulties with product structures.

The survey participants were asked, 'Does exposure to any one structural type for any length of time influence the attitudes of staff and management within the organisation?' In rapidly changing, or opportunistic, markets, product-structured organisations are identified as too inflexible. Essentially, they are slow to adapt their array of products and services to changing market conditions. Furthermore, product structures seem to stimulate a predominant style of management. The survey results show that management and staff do just what is required. Upward influence would be considered unacceptable. Downward influence relies on communicating what tasks and responsibilities are to be undertaken, with the expectation that these would then be implemented.

Furthermore, most responses emphasised that living and working in product-structured organisations generates strong predominant attitudes. Greater respect for authority is observed. A significant sentiment to have repeatedly emerged from the survey was, 'There is a right and a wrong way of doing things.' Senior managers also hold it important that lower-level management and staff be tidy and ordered. Great emphasis is given to attention to details, at times to the exclusion of strategic considerations. Principally, focus is on the task at hand rather than the nature of relationships with others in the different parts of the business.

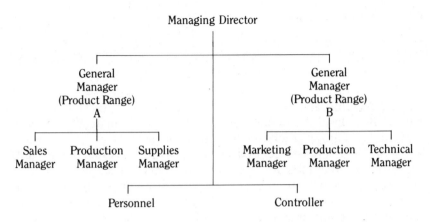

Figure 3.2 *Product structure*

Universities are essentially product-structured organisations, as are certain of the large and well-known engineering companies. The attention to quality of services or products and to the technical aspects of the job is observable. The inability to respond to change is equally well pronounced. In certain product-structured organisations, change is resisted to the point where it must be imposed. Under such circumstances, defensiveness and rigidity of response to the changing external world emerge as the coping strategies. Unless an enlightened management is directing a product-structured organisation, change may induce a feeling of fighting against insurmountable odds.

Such an enlightened management directs SC Johnson Wax Professional. Johnson Wax Professional is undergoing a major reorganisation of the company's European structure, by emphasising Europe as the region, and not the individual countries, through an integrated services (product) stream structure. In this way, key services, such as food processing or building services, should be able to provide a consistently high standard of service throughout Europe. Under the able leadership of Gary Konarske, vice-president and regional director, who is well aware of the pitfalls of regionalising and then on top of that creating service streams (product structure), the programme of change seems to be a success. Most noticeable is the positive and open attitude of the senior managers in Gary's team. Consistently high standards are expected by SC Johnson Wax Professional customers, for instance, McDonalds. Whether in Milton Keynes or Moscow, SC Johnson Wax Professional is committed to providing a high level of service.

Divisional structure

Divisional structure (Figure 3.3) involves dividing the organisation into separate and, at times, virtually autonomous units each of which provides a comprehensive range of products or services to any one customer group. Divisional structures often arise when an organisation has to be sub-divided into smaller units, termed divisions or subsidiaries, each having at its head divisional directors or subsidiary managing directors reporting to a group chief executive. Each division may be configured as a functional, product-structured, or even matrix-structured organisation. The principal functions of corporate headquarters are strategic planning, appraisal of policies and projects, and overall financial control, leaving each division a certain latitude to adopt its own approaches to sales and marketing, the hiring and development of its personnel, and the further penetration of its existing customer bases. Strategic alliances, joint ventures, and penetrating new customer bases are undertakings that need to be negotiated with corporate headquarters. Essentially, a divisional structure should focus on corporate strategy, and the business units below should be concerned with business strategy.

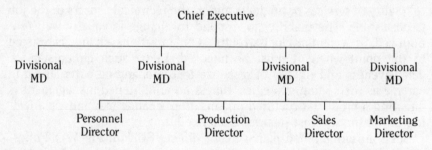

Figure 3.3 *Divisional structure*

Effective decision making and the management of a divisional structure depend partly on the quality of data concerning long-term market trends, consumer behaviour, the behaviour of competitors, national and international political issues, and the quality of management information. systems within the divisions and between the centre and the divisions, but, crucially, also on the quality of executive relationships between the group CEO and the divisional MDs. In fact, until one penetrates that upper circle, it is impossible to discover what really drives the organisation, the combination of personalities within that senior grouping or economic and business logic (see 'Best practice inventory', Chapter 2).

Case Study 3.1

WHERE TO PLACE R & D?

A multinational, divisionally structured organisation producing chemical products, most of which service the agricultural market, faced an interesting dilemma concerning where to position R & D for agricultural products. The UK divisional director (agricultural products) wished to preserve and expand his own R & D facility. A powerful, overseas divisional director producing related products wished to centralise his own R & D within the UK R & D facility but under his control. The overseas director ran a far bigger division and held a seat on the corporate centre's strategic management group. The UK director held no position within this key forum, but his issues were represented by the MD of the UK operation.

The issue of the location of R & D was never fully discussed at the strategy group meetings. Both divisions, although supplying related and overlapping products, supplied different regions of the world. Maintaining a separation of R & D, at least on the issue of product customisation, made sense. Furthermore, the UK divisional director had gone to substantial lengths to integrate R & D on particular product lines common to both divisions. His efforts were recognised and appreciated. To complicate the scenario, the MD of the UK operation was a trusted and respected figure who controlled a large proportion of the business. He firmly signalled that despite the duplication of R & D costs, product quality and customer satisfaction were better serviced by the two separate facilities. The UK MD clearly showed his support for his own divisional director.

The issue remained unresolved, creating division and bad feeling in the strategic management group, as was shown particularly in discussions concerning product quality and allocation of R & D funding. It became obvious that the R & D facility within the UK division was of the highest quality, producing value-added products suitable for manufacture and sale, while the other R & D unit was, professionally speaking, suspect and, at times, required the assistance of the UK staff to help with certain problems. In terms of utilisation, the UK facility was near capacity, while the other was seen as overmanned and expensive in overhead. Under these circumstances, the UK director displayed his displeasure, when he considered that an R & D contract which should have been allocated to his unit was allocated to the other unit, by talking openly to his own management and staff of the 'inhibiting politics coming out of New York and that *other place!*'

What started as an irritant became a substantial underlying discomfort within the strategy group. The market for agricultural products had grown substantially. More competitive customised products began to flood the market. The issue of R & D was no longer of tactical, but of strategic importance. The intensity of debate between the UK MD and the overseas divisional director increased dramatically, not just on issues of funding allocation, but also on the integration of R & D. The principle behind integration was cost saving – that made sense. Where to place the R & D facility became a political debate. At one meeting, the underlying sensitivities almost came to the surface when the UK MD strongly hinted that the new integrated R & D operation should be housed where the skills were, not where the underutilised costs existed. The other members of the strategy group stiffened as the overseas director politely but bitterly asked just what the statement meant. Any dialogue concerning agricultural products caused considerable strain in the group, because of the backroom lobbying of the other members of the group prior to meetings. Certainly, the others did not relish the thought of being cornered and committed to a point of view prior to the formal meeting.

It was becoming obvious that the R & D costs were too high. Furthermore, new product development, as well as customisation, would have to be the strategies for the future; in effect, a far more proactive strategic approach to R & D. Also, it was common knowledge that the UK MD was shortly to retire. The group CEO called a special management committee meeting with his key divisional directors and MDs of subsidiaries to discuss the need for a more refined R & D strategy. Corporate planning and group personnel became involved. After analysis, visiting of sites and considerable dialogue, it was decided to integrate R & D within the overseas divisional directorate. The quality of the staff and output of the UK operation was openly acknowledged. The UK R & D site would not be closed down. A slimmed-down operation would continue to exist. No staff were to be made redundant, and particularly generous packages were offered to those required to relocate abroad. The UK divisional director made his feelings plain on the issue, unwisely, some thought, as he was a candidate for the post of MD, UK. As it turned out, an external candidate was appointed to the position. The UK divisional director was offered instead the new post of director of research, a position he declined. The UK divisional director left, as did some of his better researchers. He is currently group director of research with a competitor, busy hiring some of his old staff. Currently, the integrated R & D facility in the overseas division has had to lay off some of its staff, as certain product lines have not been successful in the market-place. The issue of R & D is to be discussed at the next group management committee meeting.

Ironically, the bigger the organisation, the greater the number of divisions and operating units, and the greater the potential for personalities to determine the shape and direction of the organisation. The reason for this is that the range of responsibilities and accountabilities the group and divisional directorate have to manage is considerable. There is no reason to assume that the demands and issues within one division are synonymous with the issues of another division. Potentially different pulls and pushes may be present at the divisional/corporate interface. Under those circumstances, the maturity of the divisional MDs is a telling factor. Equally important is the loyalty of the divisional MDs – do their loyalties lie with the division/operating units or with the corporate centre? Where loyalties really lie can substantially influence the shape, direction and identity of both corporate centre policy and divisional policy. Experience strongly suggests that there is *no* reason to assume that the interests of corporate centre policy and the interests of the divisional/operating units are synonymous, or even broadly in keeping with each other. As can be seen in Case Study 3.1, a considerably different outcome would have emerged if the UK MD had adopted a broader, more corporate, more cost-based approach to the issue of R & D.

Unless one is privy to the true dialogue at the corporate/divisional interface, one will never really know the extent to which strategy is being driven by the mixture of personal chemistries. Sensitively applied people management skills are required to make divisional structures work. Ironically, the survey results show that the senior managers of divisional structures rate people skills as the least important managerial skill.

Matrix structure

Matrix structure (Figure 3.4) involves co-ordinating, through straight-line and dotted-line relationships, managers from different locations and/or specialists into the day-to-day operation of the organisation. Matrix management is simply a mechanism for generating greater flexibility over task activities and stimulating more market-responsive attitudes among managers and specialists in the organisation. A matrix structure is required when, in order to provide the products or services to the market, substantial co-ordination and interrelationships within the organisation and between organisations is required. Line control and colleague co-operation need to go hand in hand. On this basis, line and functional managers can be placed in a quandary, in that the balance between control and co-ordination may not be universally understood by the managers concerned. Managers who should utilise influencing skills in order to make dotted-line relationships work behave as line executives and, unfortunately, demotivate the management and staff with whom they interact. A demotivated and unco-operative manager in any of the three other structures can at least be told what to do. That telling style may well not work in a matrix structure. A disillusioned manager in a matrix can cause substantial harm to the business.

The distinction between a matrix organisation and a 'mess' relies on the maturity of managers and their attitude to staff, coupled with the attitude of staff towards management, especially at the key interfaces. As indicated in Chapter 5, maturity is the ability to invite, receive and handle feedback. The opportunity to facilitate a *feedback relationship* at key interfaces is crucial to the effective functioning of a matrix structure. In Figure 3.4, the new business development function is able to contribute effectively *only* if the problems, concerns and challenges of each of the four areas are appreciated. That means that an open and honest dialogue has to begin at those four interfaces. The balance that has to be struck at each of those four interfaces involves respecting the position and views

97

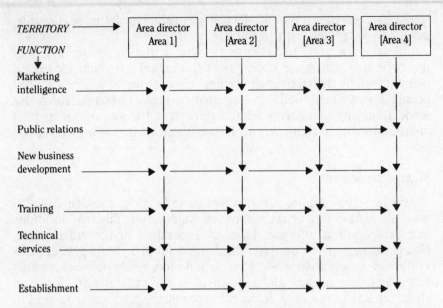

Figure 3.4 *Matrix structure*

of each of the area directors, while at the same time assisting them to rethink their local strategy to take into account new business development opportunities. The *business wisdom* of the managers at those interfaces, be they line managers or support/functional managers, is under scrutiny (see Chapter 4 for details on making interfaces work). The personality and style of the managers, their ability to form an acceptable conclusion from possibly different perspectives, distinguishes the matrix from a mess. In a matrix-structured organisation, staff and managers are more exposed to each other without necessarily having the fall-back position of authority to determine action. The effective management of a matrix structure is considerably influenced by the 'chemistry' and interaction of a considerable number of people at more than one interface. Training staff and management alike to make the matrix structure work is a prerequisite for long-term success.

The survey results illustrate that to compete with organisations facing high-performing competitors who are customer responsive, you should apply a matrix configuration in your organisation. In well-managed matrix organisations, senior and middle managers are more likely to be business-performance oriented. Through their having to interrelate on both a straight-line and a dotted-line basis with others in different parts of the organisation, their awareness as to what performance is required to induce competitive advantage is heightened.

SHAPING THE BUSINESS

I've worked in a matrix structure – never again.

Director, manufacturing, multinational organisation,
printing industry

In this sort of organisation [functionally structured] no one ever talks to each other.

Director, finance, mid-sized corporate, textile industry

Numerous comments made by senior executives in the case studies and the survey, concerning the problems they face in making their structures operate effectively, gave the impression that particular types of structures are more difficult to operate than others. Analysis indicates the contrary! Identifying the overall structural configuration is important, in order to provide a focus and identity to attain goals and objectives. As already indicated, particular styles and attitudes among staff do emerge the longer one sort of organisational structure is maintained in operation. The research highlights participants' views on the limitations of a product-structured organisation.

However, research also shows that the issue is not just the type of structure, but more the means by which organisational structures are administered. Shaping the business to perform effectively involves paying attention to four factors which strongly influence the effective working of the structure – namely clear identification of the structure, clear identification of targets, clear definition of responsibilities, and knowing the job.

Clear identification of the structure

Clearly identifying the structure involves a twofold process: recognising the nature of the present structure and identifying the desired structure for the future. Consideration of structures is vital. If the structure does not focus resources and attention on the attainment of particular targets, then the organisation will not be inducing the desired level of revenue. Structures need to be changed, as circumstances change. The skill is in knowing what one has, what one should have, and how often change should be introduced, bearing in mind the attitudes and limitations of one's staff and management.

Clearly identify the present structure of the organisation. In practice, it is unlikely that the structure of an organisation clearly matches any one of the four structural blueprints. Depending on the size of the organisation and on the role and interrelationship of the support functions to the line operating units, structural configurations evolve to suit the business needs, custom and practice of each organisation. It is possible to develop a functional or product-structured organisation with an underlying regional structure. Is such a structure, in reality, one of function or product, or has the structure changed to a matrix pattern without senior managers being aware of such an evolution? Is the present structure sufficiently robust for management to be aware of, and up to date on, the needs and requirements of customers, suppliers, distributors, and external agents who may be key channels to the market, and to respond accordingly? Does the present structure enhance or inhibit internal co-operation and cross-linkages, which are necessary to provide the best possible resources for the customer/market interface? – in effect, is territorialism frowned upon, or, in reality, accepted? Does the structure stimulate more positive or negative attitudes in terms of communication patterns, and levels of trust across and up and down the organisation? An understanding of structure and a sensitivity to the culture(s) within the organisation will provide the answer.

Recognising the nature of the present structure is important in order to appreciate whether the current configuration is conducive to addressing the business needs of the organisation. It is important to recognise what advantages or limitations are being imposed on the business performance of the organisation. In my experience, most senior managers can, relatively clearly, state what type of structure is currently in operation, its limitations, and its impact on the attitudes and behaviours of the staff and management. However, substantially fewer could name the type of structure that may be required in the future. Furthermore, only a small minority can name the different types of organisation structure blueprints.

In seminars, workshops, conferences, and in the Cranfield surveys, the question asked was, How many different types of organisation structure blueprints exist? The responses varied from one type to infinity!

Considerable ignorance exists at senior levels concerning structures. Knowledge of the different structural types, of their advantages and limitations, and of their impact on people does not trip off the tongue. Hence, although many senior managers may recognise the nature of their present structure, the same degree of clarity does not emerge when they consider the structural configuration for the future. The assumptions senior managers make about the role of key functions, the requirements of key managerial levels, the necessary linkages across the organisation, the personal qualities of senior managers required to occupy key positions, and managing the process of change may be in-accurate and unrealistic. A problem seems to exist concerning knowledge of structures and the skill to adapt and change structures to suit new business, political and social circumstances.

It is as important to recognise the present structural design, as it is to appreciate intimately the structural configuration for the future. Not to be so acquainted with structures means that boxes and lines are being drawn and redrawn on paper with little impact in practice. However, the FI Group is an exception.

> In the early days, the FI Group had developed a regional structure with a small headquarters staff. That was fine when the company was essentially dealing with local customers. At the time, the company was at its entrepreneurial stage, and the regions needed autonomy to grow. However, the point at which I arrived was interesting, for the market was changing and changes were needed in the structure and organisation of the Group.
>
> I considered it important for us to grow nationally to meet the needs of a maturing and more sophisticated market. Also, the technology for building software was beginning to change and we knew that considerable investment would be needed in both software and hardware to keep ourselves up-to-date. So functions had to be pulled into the middle, such as the sales activity, and a central marketing and central technology unit were created. The reasons for reorganisation should always be to meet the business needs of the company and to respond to the changes in the external environment. Essentially, we broke up the regional organisation and reorganised the company into a centrally controlled functional matrix. Although it was a difficult change process, requiring new management skills to work the more intricate relationships, the reorganisation really worked. We have successfully competed with organisations considerably bigger than ourselves and have almost tripled turnover within a four-year period. We have now entered into the next phase, breaking down the matrix and creating separate business units. How far we will go down this road remains to be seen.

> Hilary Cropper,
> Chief Executive,
> FI Group

Hilary Cropper heads an interesting organisation. Founded by Mrs Steve Shirley, the FI group has grown rapidly to become a major player in the computer software industry. Most of its employees are women, both in management and in the provision of software services and skills. Some work from the office and some work from home. Under these circumstances, Hilary Cropper is well aware of what it means to change from one structural design to another. As she says,

> Thinking structures is really nothing unusual for me. When I was at
> ICL we needed to be familiar with such issues to effectively compete
> in a fast-moving systems business within a very turbulent market. I
> learnt early on that strategy and structure are intimately linked;
> what many managers don't realise is that company culture has also
> to be moulded to keep in step with them – that's the hard part!

For Hilary Cropper, bedding down the structure requires planning, fore-
sight and attention to people in order to make the reorganisation work!
The flexible work patterns that the FI group have evolved can now be
held up as a model for a practical approach to working.

Clear identification of performance targets

Clearly identify the performance targets to be pursued by the operating
units and the support functions. Clearly identifying targets is basic. By
so doing, staff and management understand what each department or
function is aiming to achieve. Clarifying the targets makes it possible to
focus jobs and structure individual responsibilities to attain those goals.

The responsibility for identifying the goals to be attained for each
department or function falls on the departmental or functional head and
his boss. The targets could be financial, in terms of costs and expenditure; sales and revenue; or volume and type of products to be discharged
into the market. Time itself could be a target. For the larger corporate
consultancies, such as KPMG Peat Marwick McLintock, Coopers &
Lybrand Deloitte, and Price Waterhouse, a common topic of conversation is *utilisation*. What are the utilisation targets for the next period of
time? Fundamentally, utilisation refers to the amount of time a consultant can book to a fee-paying job.

Hence, in target setting, it is important to identify what needs to be
attained over what period of time. In certain organisations, targets are
agreed after a dialogue between two senior managers, whereby issues
such as market conditions, costs, and likely revenue sources and streams
have been examined. The alternative is for senior managers to set the
targets to be achieved, in keeping with the goals and objectives that they
have identified. Certainly, a dialogue, and then agreement of a target, is
viewed as the more motivating of the two arrangements.

A top-down target-setting strategy will also be effective as long as the
targets set are *realistic*. Targets set that are unrealistic considerably
undermine the morale of middle- and lower-level managers and staff. If
the top-down strategy is adopted, and departmental managers feel the
targets are unrealistic, a feeling of resignation that little else can be done
other than try, will emerge. If, however, after a dialogue between the

departmental head and the boss, unrealistic targets are set, a frustration and anger may emerge which can disrupt the relationship between the two, and will certainly influence negatively the departmental head's will to motivate and push departmental staff to attempt to attain those targets.

Hence, what is and is not a realistic target depends on the goals and objectives set by the top team, and on the effective communication of those goals and objectives down the line in order to inform middle-level management of the need for particular targets (see Chapter 4). Research indicates that the ability of the top team to generate a positive environment within the organisation, in which the objectives/goal-setting process, the communication of those objectives, and the linking of performance targets to the goals, are trusted, is crucial. If sensitivities exist within the top team whereby key business and organisational issues remain unaddressed, the more unclear the goals and objectives are, the less effective the performance-target-setting process.

The greater the contradiction between the goals set for the financial year and the behaviour of top management during that year, the greater the problems for performance targeting. If the goals set by the top are viewed as unclear or contradictory, then cross-linkages between departments or units will not be respected. Under such conditions, if the performance targets set involve a degree of interfacing across the organisation, then it is likely that poor cross-functional relations will develop. The level of trust among management and that between management and staff is likely to be low. Accusations of poor co-operation between departments and an unwillingness to support each other can become common within the organisation. Such circumstances allow for the emergence and practice of power-oriented, disruptive management styles. Although the symptoms of poor performance targeting emerge as people problems, the cause is that little attention is being given to the shaping of the business at a higher level. Not unnaturally, the survey participants emphasise that the future of the company is affected.

Clear definition of responsibilities

- Is the work content of managers' roles clearly defined?

- Are the areas of accountability in managers' roles clearly defined?

- Do managers recognise and agree to their areas of responsibility?

Clarifying each manager's areas of responsibility, recognising what activities need to be addressed and what tasks have to be accomplished, and clearly identifying the resources available to attain particular objectives, are fundamental requirements in running a business. Not to specify meaningfully what individuals are required to do, and what resources are to support them, makes it difficult to know what work needs to be done by whom and whether the effort required to focus on attaining long-term goals can be sustained.

Managers were asked, what are the respective implications of clearly defining and poorly defining job responsibilities? The results are summarised in Table 3.1 below.

Table 3.1 *Job responsibilities: the views of managers*

Poorly defined responsibilities	*Clearly defined responsibilities*
■ Control over cash flow is poor	■ Disciplined staff and management
■ Poor discipline in attending meetings	■ Higher tolerance for people
■ More time on administration than customers	■ Higher levels of feedback
■ Internal systems and disciplines are seen as synonymous with bureaucracy	■ Positive attitude to change
■ Lose track of new initiatives	■ Ownership of the job
■ Job dissatisfaction	■ Openness of style
■ Self-orientation rather than team orientation	■ More supportive senior management
■ Staff turnover	■ Job satisfaction
	■ Greater follow-through

An organisation that has not paid sufficient attention to clarifying and appropriately structuring jobs, faces a number of problems. Control over cash flow becomes problematic – a number of managers commented, 'Money is wasted in this organisation.' Controls, internal systems and discipline are seen as synonymous with bureaucracy; hence, little respect is given to the application of controls. Too much is left to managers to argue on behalf of particular projects or policies, but who lack the support of the internal systems and administration to ensure quality control. Not unnaturally, senior managers emphasise that they lose track of new initiatives. Their time is devoted to fruitless administration, attempting to track and control projects, initiatives, or, generally, levels of spending – activities which should be undertaken by lower-level personnel. Discipline overall is poor, especially in terms of attendance at meetings.

Working in such an environment does affect staff morale. A culture of being self-oriented becomes established. Respect for a team approach is minimal. In certain organisations, we found both senior and middle-level managers to be ignorant of the advantages of developing a team approach. They had never really experienced working in a clearly structured, team-based environment, and, hence, they were dismissive of alternative ways of working.

Case Study 3.2

EXPANDING THE EUROPEAN BUSINESS

A US multinational in the hi-tech communications industry had made a strategic decision considerably to expand its European business. The company had recognised that with the maturing of the US market, it could not otherwise sustain its profitability and growth plans for the forthcoming decade. After a number of false starts which involved changes of senior personnel and restructuring, Ciarron Murphy was appointed European president.

Ciarron's message to his organisation was *be flexible* – we've got the products and the expertise – we've just not sufficiently penetrated the various customer bases already identified throughout Europe.

A combined strategy of direct selling and indirect selling through distribution channels was devised. A number of strategic alliances and joint ventures were agreed between the company and different distributor networks.

The European organisation, although it had functions of both sales and marketing, adopted a strong sales philosophy in its business practice. Penetrating the customer base meant getting to know clients well and attempting to be as client responsive as possible. To aid the process, Ciarron, the ex-European sales director, also 'went on the road', forming strong relationships with key executives in the mid-to-large-sized corporations in Europe. Inevitably, most key clients wanted to relate to the top man – Ciarron – a process which he allowed to take place.

As the principal concern was to sell, the distinction between sales and marketing became blurred. As certain clients spanned national boundaries across a number of European countries, different salespersons ended up dealing with the same client, at times competing with each other in order to improve their own bottom line. No adequate procedures were devised for the transfer of a client from one salesperson to another, or to the local distributor, should the needs of the client require switching personnel.

The inevitable soon occurred. As selling had grown to depend so much on the quality of relationship between client and salesperson, clients learnt how to negotiate on price through manipulating the relationship between themselves and the salesperson. For identical hardware or software products, different clients were purchasing the same products at substantially different prices. Soon other clients became aware of the price differentials and complained. The complaints reached the ears of the corporate CEO, who intervened in the affairs of the European subsidiary by stating that he wanted the new VP, marketing (Europe) to be a US appointee from corporate headquarters.

Throughout this period, staff turnover, especially of sales staff, was high. During one exceptional period of six months, sales staff turnover stood at 56 per cent, a damaging experience, especially as the sales philosophy of the business was based on establishing and nurturing personal contacts.

It did not take long for the new VP, marketing to find himself in conflict with his boss, the European president. The style of both men, although abrasive, was not the prime cause of tension. Their different attitudes to managing the business were the cause. The new VP, marketing, was disciplined, and structured his department to pursue clearly identified goals. By so doing, he naturally objected to the practice of suiting the prices and products to customers. He also objected to the considerable overlap and duplication of activities between the sales and marketing functions.

The VP, marketing, is having an impact on Ciarron in that greater clarity and discipline between the sales and marketing functions has been introduced. The differential pricing practice has been stopped. The tension between the two men, however, is now greater than ever.

How, exactly, the situation will sort itself out is unclear.

The staff turnover problem in Ciarron's organisation in Case Study 3.2 has still today not been adequately addressed, despite the efforts of the VP marketing. It seems likely that Ciarron will be moved to another part of the organisation in order to allow the process of clarifying the structure and job responsibilities to take place. Although the problems of the European operation are well understood by most senior managers, Ciarron has an enviable sales track record, and corporate headquarters does not wish to lose him.

Organisations that have established clearly structured jobs, and that are well balanced in terms of responsibilities and accountabilities, tend to stimulate a more positive culture towards the business and the organisation. Greater personal discipline is displayed by senior managers in terms of attending meetings, jointly pushing the same message down the line, and being effective at follow-through. With executives recognising what is expected of them, the atmosphere in the company becomes more open. Individual managers display a far greater tolerance for others, and a greater openness of style, and there is a more supportive top management which is more accessible in terms of discussing problems and, overall, is more sensitive to the need for ownership.

A recent article in the *Sunday Times* (25 March 1990) by David Quarmby, joint managing director of Sainsbury, outlines the Sainsbury experience of restructuring not only management jobs but also weekly-paid jobs. A bottom-up approach was undertaken to the analysis of jobs, with the end result that not only were certain anomalies in jobs removed, but also staff are now more fairly paid. Although the wages bill has increased, so has an understanding of the competencies required for particular jobs, an understanding which is nurtured in staff training programmes. Similarly, the relationship with the Union of Shop, Distributive and Allied Workers, which recently withdrew an equal-value claim on seeing the results of the job restructuring, is now reported to be improved.

Clearly structuring jobs by focusing on key responsibilities not only helps staff to improve performance in their jobs, but also stimulates a more positive attitude to the organisation.

Know the job

How long should a person remain in post? Moving a manager too soon from his job could mean transferring him while he is still in his learning curve. The manager has not made a sufficient contribution and is also pushed into a second learning curve before he has fully emerged from the first. (See Chapter 1 – the transition curve.)*

There is also the fear that if a manager is in the same job for too long, he becomes stale. He becomes too accustomed to his surroundings. He is too comfortable and lacks the will and insight to change and adapt his organisation should evidence so indicate. The issue of tenure of placement is as much relevant to middle as to senior management.

The results indicate considerably wide bands of time on placement, ranging from one to ten years. However, from the point of view of effectiveness, a minimum placement time of five years has emerged as the key finding. The results also indicate that rather than becoming stale and demotivated, a manager becomes more effective the longer he stays in the job, up to the ten-year point. Hence, the guideline to emerge is that placement in a senior management role should last from five to ten years, adjusted according to the nature of the job, the manager's willingness to change, and his level of personal ambition.

If effectiveness improves the longer the manager remains in post (see Table 3.2), to what does effectiveness refer?

*Although the learning required to become effective once appointed to a new job, and the length of tenure are linked issues, they are treated in this book as separate topics. For senior managers, being in transition has vision implications, and length of tenure influences how the structure is utilised in terms of sustained marketplace penetration. For middle management, research indicates that such a sharp distinction does not apply.

Table 3.2 *Impact of years in the job: results of research*

Issue	Impact
■ Understanding and influencing the organisation structure	*Greater* the nearer to 10 years in the job
■ Trust and tolerance	*Greater* the nearer to 10 years in the job
■ Follow-through	*Greater* the nearer to 10 years in the job
■ Attention to detail and discipline	*Greater* the nearer to 10 years in the job
■ Outlook and awareness of issues	*Greater* the nearer to 10 years in the job
■ Understanding of customers, competition and improving profitability	*Greater* the nearer to 10 years in the job

Added value to be gained from placement in the job relates to knowing how to operate in the structure, how to manage follow-through, attention to detail, general awareness of internal and external issues, and understanding and responding to customers' needs.

Understanding the configuration of the structure and knowing how to influence individuals and groups within the structure improves the longer a manager spends in the job. Straight-line reporting relationships are relatively easy to comprehend, and the information as to who reports to whom is available on organisation charts. Managing dotted-line relationships is more difficult, especially if such relationships do not appear on paper (see Chapter 4 for information on nurturing interfaces). Influencing the structure means influencing people who hold key roles in the structure. It takes time to get to know these people; it takes time to recognise how to relate to them, especially if the organisation is, in reality, run on a web of dotted-line relationships. Other staff also have to become acquainted with the manager and the way he thinks and operates. The chances of establishing an effective and positive working relationship improve with time. Trust in each other, tolerance of each other, and simply becoming known in a mid-to-large-sized corporate business organisation can take years to establish.

Oil companies and the clearing banks tend to have a well-established, internal, old boy network. It is an unwritten law that at the start of any in-company, senior management development programme (tailor-made for the managers of one company), time has to be made for reminiscence and talking about old times. Not to do so could disrupt the programme. Hence, most management development programmes start on a Sunday evening with as much time spent talking and socialising as preparing for the programme. However, this evolving club culture is not negative. If we bear in mind that one crucial finding of this survey is that the quality of executive relationships can enhance or damage the business, we can see that how senior managers relate to each other is of vital concern. The longer senior managers have known each other, the more they have worked together, and the more they understand each other's job-related problems and issues, the more supportive they are likely to be of each other, and, equally, the more open the style of communication. People who have known each other for some time, and who have appreciated the nature of each other's role problems, contact each other in terms of asking for advice or offering assistance. Within such an environment, the crucial and sensitive issue of transferring resources is considerably less problematic. It is therefore important to ensure that familiarity does not lead to complacency.

Longer placement in the job provides advantages in terms of relating to not only colleagues and bosses, but also to subordinates. Attention to follow-through is crucial if control is to be maintained over new developments and initiatives. Follow-through involves being kept informed of progress on projects and decisions being implemented; in fact, being kept regularly informed on how initiatives are proceeding. Much depends on the quality of relationships in order for effective follow-through to take place. Well-known and respected senior managers report that before any new project or initiative gets under way, they obtain agreement on how they are to be kept informed of developments. Certain managers organise periodic meetings, others go walkabout, and still others rely on seemingly casual meetings to ask questions concerning progress. Interestingly, the skills of being able to handle people are not sufficient. A manager's being known, understood and respected has emerged as the feature most conducive to follow-through.

Managers not so long in the job, especially under two years, and probably not fully appreciating the issues and concerns of colleagues and managers lower in the organisation, report that they find the systems and administration in the organisation a hindrance, and that they relate best to managers who have come from a similar technical background. In effect, the manager has not really settled into the job, has not made his contacts, and has not made himself sufficiently well known, and is finding the system constraining.

Effective follow-through requires personal discipline, an attention to detail, and an acquaintance with the people in order to establish the necessary credibility and trust.

> Well, I ask a lot of questions . . . If I go through a plant, which I do from time to time, they now know I always ask one or two questions they can't answer and they know that if I don't get an answer in a week they get a reminder, so it's a sort of, I hope, constructive but certainly demanding relationship. But I have a standard rule that I never communicate instructions to people in the business, I always go through the Managing Director of the business. I come back and I send a note saying, I think you should do so and so. Generally they do. I think there's a great danger of confusing relationships, so when I go round plants, I ask information questions and get answers on them, but if that leads to any conclusions, or if I find someone who's not really up to the mark, I take that back through the Managing Director. Otherwise people see a double-headed authority, and then you get groups and cabals and conspiracies.
>
> Lord Tombs of Brailes,
> Chairman,
> Rolls Royce plc

The capacity to talk in a comfortable manner, and the personal discipline to ensure that questions are answered, while respecting organisational relationships, certainly makes for a formidable top manager. Lord Tombs, in interview, emphasised the importance he attributes to managing people, and the time he makes to get to know staff. These, he said, were among the measures allowing him properly to discharge his responsibilities as chairman of Rolls Royce plc.

Hand in hand with understanding the internal organisational dynamics, the longer-established senior manager develops a growing appreciation of the market and economic issues that face his company. Those senior executives who have been in the job for over five years display an understanding of how to focus more effectively on customer groups, how to hold meaningful discussions concerning competitor impact, and how to deliver goods or services on time. In terms of managing people, their managers display greater proficiency in the handling of competitors, and, overall, staff are better motivated, as measured by fewer resignations and transfers.

The survey results indicate that those senior managers who are longer in post develop a broader outlook and a heightened awareness as to the issues they face. Managers do not become stale and underperform simply because they have held the same job for any length of time. A great deal depends on the length of tenure, how clearly structured is the role, how clearly defined are the goals, how effective are the internal communication processes, and how stimulating are the people and the working environment.

Do the organisation charts capture reality?

■ On the company's organisation charts, what sorts of relationships are portrayed?

■ Are the straight-line relationships, as well as the key dotted-line relationships, fully outlined?

■ Do the organisation charts capture the reality of the way business is conducted?

The more representative the organisation chart is of the reality of the straight-line and the dotted-line relationships required to make the structure work, the clearer staff and management within the organisation will appreciate the nature of their jobs, in relation to those with whom they need to interrelate in order to work. If the relationships necessary to undertake work are complex, then it may be appropriate to explore whether such relationships can be simplified. If not, then those key relationships necessary for the effective functioning of the structure should be clearly drawn out and generally made available.

It is unwise, especially in a matrix-structured organisation, to attempt falsely to simplify relationships by identifying only the key functional relationships. For staff and management, such organisation charts are meaningless. They do not capture the reality of their working experience, nor assist their understanding of which relationships may require greater attention, in order better to achieve objectives and attain higher standards of work. On seeing poorly configured organisation structure charts, staff and lower-level management are less likely to trust top management's ability to be in touch with their reality. Personnel from the lower levels are likely to respond with,

> Just another organisation chart – so what – makes no difference in any case. Those guys up there don't know what the hell is happening.
>
> Managing consultant,
> large corporate consultancy

A positive orientation towards organisation structures is captured in the two following comments.

111

A structure is the way that messages are transmitted through the organisation, the way that people are directed, particularly inasmuch as a structure will affect the way a company behaves externally, and the more that anomalies in the structure are perceived in the marketplace, and if that causes people to behave in a confused manner vis-a-vis the marketplace, then that clearly will hurt the organisation and impair its ability to be effective.

Carol Ward,
Human Resources Director,
Square D (Europe) Corporation

The clearer the structure, the more the degree of consistency, even though there is divergence between Manchester and Kent. It's the degree to which the people concerned get together to talk, understand each other and where the structure focuses their attention in dealing with that problem.

Tom Frost,
CEO,
NatWest Bank

Tom Frost should know. The massive reorganisation of NatWest, termed Carnation, which is taking the overheads and putting them into the earnings division, is working. 'It is producing ... arguments and debates, such as I have not seen before over the last ten years, through our management team.'

Draw the organisation structure the way it is truly intended to work and the way personnel have been focused.

BEST PRACTICE INVENTORY

Dos

☐ Know about structures. Organisation structures are the means by which resources are focused to achieve goals and targets. Thus, structures are a powerful influence on attitudes and behaviours. The structure strongly influences patterns of behaviour by emphasising desired practices and processes directed towards particular ends. Hence, appreciating the current structural configuration, its strengths, and its weaknesses allows top management realistically to appraise what changes need to be introduced if change is required.

☐ Make performance targeting realistic. As stated, performance targeting can be conducted through discussion between senior management and departmental heads or through a top-down process. Whichever of the two avenues is utilised, the targets set must be realistically achievable. In certain situations, resistance to increased performance is to be expected and understandable. However, if experience shows that certain targets are unattainable, management and staff can become seriously demoralised. Trust in top management's ability to be realistic will be seriously eroded.

☐ Clearly structure jobs so that staff are in no doubt about what they are required to do, know where their responsibilities lie, and recognise what they will be held accountable for. Balancing responsibilities with accountabilities is necessary if general managers are to be motivated to display unity with the top team. Substantial responsibility with little accountability induces a poor sense of self-discipline or maturity, as managers are given considerable freedom to do what they want with no comeback. Alternatively, jobs that have few responsibilities but considerable accountabilities, induce conservative, non-risk-taking behaviour. Under such circumstances, managers have little control over what others do. However, managers need to feel directly responsible for resources which are under their control, so that the process of performance assessment (being held to account) is seen to be equitable.

☐ Review current job-placement practice. Especially for senior managerial roles, moving personnel off the job too soon may mean taking them out of the role while in their learning curve. It takes time to learn how to 'manipulate' the structure. Similarly, it takes time to know how to interact externally with key clients or support services, such as suppliers and distributors, so that one can effectively interact with them. Research indicates that placements, for key roles, of not fewer than five years are necessary in order to make a positive impact.

☐ Make jobs attractive and stimulating. Increasing the length of time in the job does not automatically mean that the manager becomes stale and underperforms. The amount of challenge and interest built into the job and the support given to staff, strongly influence personal performance.

Don'ts

☐ Do not assume that short-term placements are valuable, except in crisis situations. Especially for expatriate placements, becoming acquainted with the local culture, recognising what sales and marketing really mean in local regional markets, and having the confidence to provide accurate cost and revenue forecasts to corporate headquarters takes time. The practice of certain multinational and international companies of two-year placements tends to be unproductive and, at times, destructive. Local management may end up resenting corporate headquarters' insensitivity to local problems, and this may lead to lost opportunities in that market.

Recognising what structure is required is half the story. Knowing then how to manage the structure induces added-value performance. Organisation structure is one important medium for *spreading the message.*

PART II
INFLUENCING SKILLS

What I have tried to do is force the team concept through . . .
I think to get a good team going, you have got to share things,
you have to share information and be good at handling feedback
as well.

Colin Sharman,
Senior South East Regional Partner,
KPMG Peat Marwick McLintock

PART II

INTERVIEWING SKILLS

4

Spreading the Message

It seems to me the whole thing is trying to persuade people down the line – This is your unit. You manage it the way you think best. We'll agree with you what the objectives are, and there are bound to be some rules, because you can't invent your own banking system ... but within that you can do your own thing. You can decide which products you can sell more of and which you are not going to bother with. You may, in some areas, have pricing discretion ... So there will be rules, but at least we try to articulate what they are, and where there aren't rules you do your own thing. Perhaps most importantly, where you don't think the rules are right, tell your boss and negotiate a change.

Mark Hely Hutchinson,
Ex-Chief Executive Officer,
Bank of Ireland

The Bank of Ireland has evolved a particularly innovative philosophy for effectively managing people in order to manage change. From, in the early 1980s, a traditional domestic bank, beset with union problems, a decreasing market share running at a rate of 1 per cent per year, and increasing cost problems, it is now a far better performing organisation offering a wide range of financial services. It has changed its culture to be more professional and customer sensitive. The bank also has its own building society, an insurance company, a bank in the US, and a substantial presence in the UK.

Is there a secret to the bank's success? Not really – for Mark Hely Hutchinson, with his senior managers, had placed high emphasis on managing people. By that, the senior managers did not mean being polite, sensitive or charming. They believe in, and project, core business values which are crucial to the growth and development of the bank, as much during Mark's period of stewardship, as after his departure. In his words, 'We have made a lot of internal play with slogans like *Freedom To Manage* – which I believe in very strongly.' For the Bank of Ireland, the policy of growth through people has worked, and its success was publicly acknowledged in 1989, when the bank was awarded the Service Quality

Award for Ireland. The Bank of Ireland has recognised that it is of paramount importance to *spread the message*.

WHAT MESSAGE?

What message should be spread? The only answer to that question is to ask what values epitomise, or should epitomise, your business?

What are business values?

Business values are the fundamental beliefs underlying the business with which staff and management identify!

■ Is the customer important?

■ Are people important?

■ What about quality of service?

Experience indicates that when asked such questions, the vast majority of responses are in the affirmative – of course, these things are important.

What counts, however, is behaviour! Identifying a set of values that are crucial to the growth of the business and meaningful to both staff and management, and then communicating those values, are two sides of the same coin. It does matter what people say. What they *do*, however, counts more. Do management and staff *behave* in ways that exhibit the values of customer- and quality-of-service orientation? All organisations evolve fundamental beliefs and values about customers, products, quality, personnel and responsiveness to the market. The range of values is limitless. Certain values are positive – care and attention are given to customers and to quality of service. Certain behaviours, however, are negative – too much attention is paid to internal concerns, rather than to knowing how to respond appropriately to customers and competitors. If such negative behaviours continue too long, they become a value – a negative value – which hurts the organisation.

Furthermore, the longer a set of beliefs and values is followed, the more those values become normal, and the more they become part of the culture of the organisation. Unless an effort has been made to recognise the nature of the more deeply held views concerning the organisation, it is common for people slowly to become unaware of the key values that determine their behaviour.

Case Study 4.1

YOU'VE GOT TO BE AS FLEXIBLE AS ME

The CEO of a box manufacturing company strongly believed in customer care and responsiveness to customer needs. This he exhibited in his personal behaviour by making himself available to meet clients, listen to their needs and problems, and respond to and accept their criticisms when things went wrong. Admirable! His working day was long, taking into account the dinners and social occasions with clients. He often started at 7.30 am and may have been home by 10.30 pm. Three or four evenings a week were spent at work.

Although his immediate subordinates and middle and senior managers respected his commitment and skills, they disliked him because he would change the time and date of meetings, his diary commitments and his subordinates' diary commitments to suit him and his particular circumstances. He would fill slots in the diaries of his directors or even attempt to change their appointments, if he wanted the team to present a public and unified front. Often he gave a week's notice; sometimes, only one day's.

Naturally, the other senior managers resented their diaries being changed so often and at such short notice, simply to suit the boss. They found it equally irritating that their meetings rarely dealt with medium- or long-term issues, but just operational matters. Meetings were not sufficiently valued, other than for addressing immediate affairs. The elder statesman on the board, a regional general manager, was not only disturbed by such behaviour, but he was also alarmed at the growing number of executives, especially the younger ones, who used the CEO as their role model. The dominant management style was one of abrupt, insensitive communication, with the net effect that crucial long-term issues were unaddressed. Not unnaturally, staff were becoming increasingly demotivated.

The regional general manager, who was shortly to retire, was a Scot who rarely held back from expressing his feelings. One day he simply refused the boss's request for an additional diary commitment.

'Why?' asked the boss. 'You told me you had nothing that day.'

'And that's the way it's going to stay,' responded the Scot. 'I need the day to catch up on crucial administration. Orders have to be pushed through the system, minutes for the next meeting have to be prepared. Most of all, I'm not going to jump simply when you decide to wave your red-hot poker around. I'm going to set a good example to my people!'

'What do you mean? Look, in this business, you've got to be as flexible as me,' responded the CEO, not hiding his irritation.

The GM told the boss exactly what he thought of him and his so-called flexibility. 'What you have, is a lack of discipline. In fact, I sometimes wonder whether all we do is respond to your anxieties,' said the GM. He also told the boss that his behaviour had now become a role model which other executives were adopting with visibly negative consequences already.

The boss, noticeably stung by such comments, listened.

Three months later, at the regional general manager's leaving party, one of the other regional general managers spoke to his retiring colleague.

'I don't know what the hell you said to him, but heaven forbid that one miss a monthly meeting, or be poorly prepared. He's even stopped putting commitments in our diaries. He always checks first. I'm not sure which is worse – him before, or him now.'

The elderly GM smiled. 'Him now is the answer. The chances are that you'll have an even harder time of it, but, definitely, the business will improve.'

The CEO of the box-making company (Case Study 4.1) was creating a culture of poor discipline, embodying the worst aspects of customer care – just jump when the customer says jump – while not acknowledging the importance of meetings and discussion of strategy. At least, the CEO had the maturity to listen. Many do not, and, by default, establish a mixed bag of negative and positive values that become embedded as the culture. Once established, such attitudes are difficult to change. 'It's the way we've always done things' is the slogan in such cultures.

HOW DO YOU SPREAD THE MESSAGE?

Frank Flynn, senior manager with responsibility for staff relations in the Bank of Ireland, has identified and utilises numerous ways for ensuring effective communication within the bank. These include walkabout, internal newsheets and newsletters, briefing groups, dinners, lunches, round tables, regular meetings – Frank's list is impressive. Still, Frank feels that something additional needs to be done. That something additional refers not only to circulating information around the system, but also to projecting the desired attitudes, values and behaviours that need to be adopted by staff and management. In effect, it is combining the techniques of communication with the practice of management.

Projecting positive, enabling values and behaviours for staff and management to adopt requires careful consideration. Communicating key values does not happen by accident; it happens by *design*. Time has to be made fully to consider and identify mechanisms for communicating, throughout the organisation, a philosophy of mind and desired behaviours to practise. Two fundamental strategies for introducing and encouraging the practice of the core values of the business are identified from research – providing direction and providing example.

Providing direction

- What does the organisation stand for?

- Where is the organisation going?

- Has a positive identity been identified and projected within and without the organisation?

These questions refer to the mission and objectives of the organisation, the two key pointers for providing direction.

Mission statement

How many organisations have a mission statement? Of those that do, how many have a mission statement which staff and management *own* and identify with. Mission statements identify the purpose, mission and identity of the organisation. The mission statement may read as if it were stating the obvious – care for clients, staff, quality and service – what counts is that within each organisation, relative to its history and culture, those statements are believed by staff and management alike.

The common practice in organisations which have mission statements is for them to be written down, as well as orally communicated by the chairman and CEO at internal management meetings and the annual company conference. Mission statements may be issued to staff either on separate sheets of paper as part of a statement from top management, or in handbooks, but an emerging practice is to issue each staff member with a small durable card identifying the key elements of the mission of the organisation. The four topics most commonly covered are customers, personnel, service and product quality, and the organisation.

Survey results indicate that 36 per cent of respondents could not identify a mission statement for their business. Of those who did, the majority recognised the danger of simply using words. The words have to mean something. 'People come first', 'customer service', 'quality of service' have now become mere catch phrases. These phrases have to be matched by actions inside the organisation which are consistent over a period of time.

Case Study 4.2

THE MANAGEMENT CONFERENCE

A multinational company in the chemicals and fertiliser business invited its top 78 managers to the annual management conference, that year held at a coastal resort

---

in Spain. The three-day event included presentations from top management, the first showing of the new company video, and certain external speakers, invited to give a presentation on topics of interest to the company. I was one of those invited speakers.

The other visiting speaker and I occupied most of the first day. Our contributions were reasonably well received. The first-day conference session closed with a presentation from the Southeast Asia regional GM, focusing on progress in Malaysia, Hong Kong and Singapore. That evening's dinner in a delightful local restaurant was followed by socialising into the early hours of the morning.

The next morning the top team was to make its presentation. The CEO began the proceedings, outlining the overall progress of the company, and stating that he would complete his speech by making the closing remarks after all the director presentations. He then introduced the next speaker, the finance director. I considered the CEO to be a clear and fluent speaker, certainly a better presenter than most I had recently witnessed. The finance director, an older man, and just as clear a communicator, seemed to be greeted by a gentle derision from the audience. The harder he tried, the more fluent his performance, the greater the antagonism from the audience. Although the questions he received at the end of his presentation were muted, the underlying hostility hung uncomfortably over the proceedings.

The manufacturing director, again an accomplished and clear speaker, spoke of the strides forward in manufacturing over the last year, and of the investments and planned progress for the next. He experienced greater hostility during his question time. I realised, observing the situation, that the audience was not 'coming clean' as to the nature of their concerns.

The CEO, observing events from the platform, quietly excused himself and slipped out of the assembly through a side door. He reappeared an hour and a half later, in time for his second speech, and made the concluding remarks on behalf of the top team. His presentation was excellent, probably the best of the conference. However, the resentment, mutterings and hostility were now greater than for any other of the senior speakers. The questioning at the end of his presentation was far more aggressive than that faced by the other presenters. This was strange, as the CEO was a popular and respected figure. His clarity as a communicator at the conference did not seem to warrant the resentment he received.

Over lunch, I listened to the comments; how awful were the presentations from top management; how unrealistic they were; this conference was a waste of time. I enquired why there were negative feelings; after all, the performance of each of the members of the top team had seemed more than adequate.

One of the senior managers at the table said, 'Yes, all right, we all know Bill [the CEO] is a good speaker, and we all like him, but how can you expect us to believe all that? That's not what we see and experience in our jobs during the year. What they [the top team] say has happened and is supposed to happen, doesn't fit with what we have seen happen or expect to happen over this coming year!'

Where events do not match words and written statements, disbelief and resentment are the result. The CEO and his colleagues (Case Study 4.2) faced the problem of wishing to improve affairs in the organisation, but they were seen as projecting key messages and values about the business and its people that were not the daily experience of the audience.

Ironically, the more professional the communication skills of the members of the top team, and the more the values projected do not match the staff's experience of what is happening in the company, the greater the hostility. Spreading the message through clearly identifying and communicating the mission of the organisation requires sensitive application in order for the mission to gain acceptance.

The survey results indicate that the internal conditions in the organisation seriously influence the projection and acceptance of the mission of the business. Under conditions of market growth in terms of penetrating new markets, or increasing market share, or operating in competitive and fast-moving markets, the level of motivation to, or receptivity from, staff and management for clearly communicating the mission, is high. Similarly, an organisation that has clearly defined goals as well as positively minded and well-motivated senior managers who adopt a management style of valuing performance vastly improves the chances of effectively communicating key values through the mission statement.

Interestingly, in function-structured organisations, the level of receptivity to concepts such as identifying with the mission statement is lower than in other types of organisation structures. The awareness as to the benefits of corporate cohesion is equally low, as emphasis is placed on attending to the concerns of each function. When interrelating is not planned to occur, why should respect be shown to corporate issues? Similarly, if senior managers adopt a style of 'do what is required', or enter into power plays with each other or lower-level management, trust and identity with the organisation are diminished, making the communication of key values almost impossible.

Communicating objectives

If the mission statement encapsulates the fundamental values and purpose of the organisation, the objectives refer to the strategic aspirations of the organisation, such as level of profitability over the next five years, or the type, or the shape and size of the organisation over the longer term. To increase market share, through strategic alliances or distributor networks, by x percentage points over the next three to five years is an example of an objective! Clearly communicating objectives, in conjunction with communicating the mission of the organisation, provides staff and management with a view of the longer-term aspirations of the company as well as an idea of what key values need to be nurtured and protected in order to provide for identity, ownership and stability among staff and management. This question was asked in the survey: Are corporate objectives clearly communicated throughout the organisation? Seventy-four per cent of respondents said yes.

Clearly communicating corporate objectives and the mission of the organisation improves morale. Staff and management adopt a positive attitude to change. They tend to be more supportive of others, to be more open in terms of management style, to display a greater commitment to the organisation, and to exhibit a greater respect for discipline and for the traditions of the organisation. Understanding where the organisation is going and what it stands for has a 'knock-on' effect, in that communications generally improve up, down and across the organisation. Ensuring effective communication becomes a way of life. Groupe Bull, in its recent restructuring, introduced an interesting innovation – a philosophy of making the top 'accessibull' to staff and management lower down. As a part of Bull's internal communication strategies promoting the restructuring programme, corporate headquarters introduced a 'telephone-in service' for personnel to ring up and pose questions about the future of Bull, or concerns for their own future, on a confidential basis. Within such a positive framework, job satisfaction improves, with the result that staff turnover decreases and loyalty to the organisation increases. When this is coupled with clear communication of the mission of the organisation, the tolerance of staff for strains and stresses, especially during periods of change, is likely to improve. The fact that positive values are inculcated by the organisation provides for greater strength and stability to weather pressure.

Table 4.1 *Communicating the mission and objectives effectively: The impact*

Corporate objectives	*Mission*
■ Improved understanding of the structure	■ Better informed
■ Greater job satisfaction	■ More positive attitude to change
■ Greater respect for discipline	■ Greater need for challenge
■ Greater respect for the traditions of the organisation	■ Greater attention to details
■ Better informed	■ Supportive of others
■ More positive attitude to change	■ Greater openness
■ Greater need for challenge	■ Higher tolerance for stress and pressure
■ Greater commitment to the organisation	
■ Greater openness	
■ Supportive of others	

Clear communication of corporate objectives is likely to promote an improved understanding of and identity with the mission and corporate structure.

> A five-year business plan. A strong budgetary control system, a highly geared and centred system, so that the goals set relate to high payments that are achieved. The goals set are fairly excessive. As a result, over the last ten years, the company has gone from total market capitalisation, valuing the company at £900m in 1979 to £9bn as of last night. So everybody who invested in 1979 has got a 31 per cent compound rate return, which is pretty high.
>
> Dr Tony O'Reilly,
> Chairman, President and CEO,
> HJ Heinz Co

In contrast to Heinz, certain organisations have placed greatest emphasis on communicating functional/departmental objectives. Time and money have not been devoted to agreeing upon and communicating the advantages of and need for a corporate identity through the corporate structure, probably as a result of tensions at senior management levels.

Alternatively, numerous organisations have placed substantial emphasis on communicating the mission statement, on plastic cards or in neatly presented handbooks issued to all staff. However, the communication of corporate objectives may be neglected. Too much is left to the discretion of subsidiary MDs, GMs or divisional and functional directors, so that inconsistency of behaviour is exhibited throughout the organisation.

As seen in Table 4.1, opposite, attention needs to be paid to the two areas of communication. It is crucial that the aspirations, values and objectives of the organisation be well integrated, effectively projected, and re-emphasised through the different internal channels of communication. Clearly to understand the mission of the organisation while experiencing inconsistency and lack of clarity as to the objectives of the organisation does little to enhance the trust of staff and management in the mission statement.

KPMG Peat Marwick McLintock, aware of the need clearly to project its corporate image (Chapter 1), also recognises the importance of communication and need for clarity of direction. The company has issued to all staff a small, neat, fold-over leaflet which not only highlights the mission statement, but also identifies the objectives and basic values of the organisation, backed by simple key questions to help consultants focus their efforts to adhere to objectives. KPMG Peat Marwick is not only communicating corporate objectives and the mission statement, but also asking its personnel what each one of them is doing to induce added value in these two areas. Are the mid-to-large-sized corporate consultancy partnerships a special case?

Those who have worked in mid-to-large-sized corporate partnerships may have the impression that their situation and problems are unique. The co-ordination issues across the partners, the short-term goal orientation, and the need constantly to attend to customer relations leave little time and room to attend to internal morale and communication problems. At least, that is what we, as a research team, were told.

Close examination of 71 consultancy and design partnerships indicates the contrary. The problems of a partnership parallel the concerns of a matrix-structured organisation. Just as in a matrix-structured business, considerable attention needs to be paid to people management and internal communications. Hence, constantly improving internal interfaces, and communicating the mission and objectives of the business, are important in such organisations. Such practices are not readily forthcoming in most partnerships. There is, however, a growing awareness of such needs in KPMG Peat Marwick. It is hardly any surprise that the professionalism of KPMG Peat Marwick is commonly acknowledged.

Providing example

■ To what extent, when commitments are made, are they followed through?

■ To what extent do the members of the top team talk about each other behind each other's backs?

■ To what extent do shouting the loudest, being pushy, and getting your own way predominate over clear and reasoned discussion?

Imagine you are attending a top-level meeting and a commitment is made by two or three senior managers to share resources and adopt a unified approach to a particular problem. After the meeting, one executive does not abide by his commitment, and no amount of reasoning by colleagues changes the situation. 'Yes, yes, yes, I'll tell my people to contact you,' he says. Afterwards, nothing happens. 'Yes, I'm sorry. I've been so busy. I've just not had the chance to respond. I'll get on to it immediately,' he says when reminded. Afterwards, nothing happens. In frustration, one or more of the colleagues retaliate by not allowing their own staff and management to co-operate with the defaulting executive. What sort of message do you think such behaviour sends down the line?

Spreading the message through more formal channels is desired. Clearly, consistently and repeatedly communicating through the written word, through walkabout, and through well-planned and well-delivered presentations is admirable and necessary. However, sustained communication that makes a positive impact on staff and management does not occur by stage managing occasions for the purposes of communication. Sustained positive communication occurs on a daily basis, in a disciplined way, in one's job, through one's behaviour.

Providing example as to the desired behaviours that lead to success is achieved by senior managers being sufficiently disciplined to practise what they preach. Providing direction and being skilled in the techniques of communication are useful. Behaving in a manner that is supportive and appropriate to the values of the organisation and the objectives being pursued is vital.

The survey participants were asked, 'What personal qualities and skills do you consider necessary to perform effectively in your role?' The results are shown in Table 4.2.

Table 4.2 *Positive executive behaviours: Survey results*

Skills	%	Qualities	%
■ *Job-related* Functional Technical	28	■ *Personality* Humour Sympathy Patience Honesty	21
■ *Personal-related* Intelligence Creativity Articulate Motivation All-round ability	9	■ *Dynamism* Forward thinking Creativity Judgement Energy/Drive Versatility	26
■ *Business-related* External issues Internal issues	14	■ *Management style* Motivating Being open with people Leadership People-oriented Customer-oriented	36
■ *People-related* People management Training and development Interpersonal skills Communication	49	■ *Inner strength* Determination Resilience Logic Discipline	17

As Table 4.1 shows, the greatest emphasis was placed on people and communication skills. Under the heading of skills, 49 per cent of responses referred to people-related skills, a substantial proportion of which covered the topic of communication. Under qualities, 36 per cent of responses referred to management style, covering such topics as motivation, leadership and an open style of management. Other job-related skills, of a functional and technical nature, such as techniques of sales and marketing and the ability to read a balance sheet, were identified as important, but were not ranked as vital. Personal qualities such as humour, patience and dynamism were attributed almost as great a value.

The general manager

A critical role in the organisation structure is the general manager. He is the meeting point between strategy and implementation. The GM is the linchpin that makes things happen! His attitudes, values and behaviours are of fundamental concern to the process of spreading the message. He is a crucial role model in providing example of positive or negative managerial practice. Spreading the message down the line involves winning over the GMs, for it is their confidence in top management that motivates them to communicate consistently and coherently the key values of the business, and to support of agreed strategy and policy.

What, then, are the predominant concerns of GMs? Three areas are identified: their views on the competence of their bosses in the top team, their perceptions of the key issues facing the business, and their predominant attitudes towards internal organisational issues.

The survey results reveal that 77 per cent of chairmen and CEOs and 61 per cent of GMs consider the top team easy to talk to! The skills of influence of top managers, their abilities to relate positively to others, and their ability to put subordinates at ease are considered to be well developed and well practised. From there on, differences of view emerge.

Sixty per cent of chairmen and CEOs consider that the members of the top team discuss sensitive issues. Only 45 per cent of GMs are of the same opinion. Sixty per cent of chairmen and CEOs consider that, as people, the members of the top team are understanding and supportive of each other. Only 34 per cent of GMs are of the same opinion. Sixty six per cent of chairmen and CEOs consider that the top team, once having made a decision, does not flinch from implementing it. Only 33 per cent of GMs are of the same opinion. The remaining 67 per cent consider that the top team implements decisions that personally suit the members concerned.

Divergence of view occurs over personnel and organisational structure issues. Eleven per cent of the responses of chairmen and CEOs indicate that the structure of the organisation is an area requiring attention, whereas 33 per cent of GMs consider structure issues to be a problem.

Greater difference of opinion exists as to whether the relationship between functions and departments is of concern – 11 per cent of the responses of chairmen and CEOs identified this as an issue, in comparison to 42 per cent of the responses from GMs. Inevitably, if differences of opinion concerning the management of the structure and the relationship of the functions and departments within the structure exist, then differences of opinion concerning the morale of people are also likely to arise. Twelve per cent of the responses of chairmen and CEOs consider the morale of employees to be an issue requiring attention. Thirty-three per cent of the responses of GMs consider morale to be a concern.

In the data on communication and control issues, 48 per cent of GMs feel they are losing track of new initiatives. Part of the problem could be that the GMs feel they are not being regularly informed, and that both divisional/subsidiary level and corporate objectives are not clearly communicated. Both groups report an awareness of the mission statement, but how, then, that is to be put into action seems to be the concern. Furthermore, 46 per cent of GMs indicate that they feel negative towards the changes that have taken place in the organisation in the recent past. Overall, 74 per cent of GMs identify or foresee one form or another of hindrance emanating from top management, to interfere with their achieving what they consider important in their current position.

Clearly, a problem exists in the relationship between top management and general management, a problem which needs to be understood if businesses are to be better run. One possible reason for such divergence is that, as a function of their roles, chairmen and CEOs are more externally focused, paying considerable attention to competitors, suppliers, distributors, government, and fluctuations in the marketplace, and hence they place a different priority on internal organisational issues. Basically, what GMs consider to be a serious problem, chairmen and CEOs do not place in such high priority.

Alternatively, it may be that chairmen and CEOs are out-of-touch with what's happening in their businesses and do not appreciate the nature of the people and organisational problems, in implementing strategy. A more likely explanation is that chairmen and CEOs are aware of the tension within their organisation but do not know how to address such concerns. What may further exacerbate the situation is the feeling that the GMs have not 'bought into' the policies and objectives of top management.

Whatever the reason, such distance between the top of the organisation and general management is a gap that needs bridging. No amount of internal PR and attention to internal communications will compensate for such a fundamental blockage in the structure. Strategies and policies are unlikely to be implemented as intended, and the morale of employees is likely to dip, with the result that staff and middle- and junior-level management will lose faith in the ability of the senior executive to manage the business. That's when staff turnover increases. The top team and the GMs must work in unison. The top team has to treat the GMs as part of the executive. A barometer of effectiveness in providing direction and example is the quality of relationship between top management and the GMs. This is one interface that requires constant nurturing if internal communications are ever to succeed.

Nurturing interfaces

Nurturing interfaces in the structure involves recognising what it means to manage straight-line and dotted-line relationships in a manner that adds value to the business.

As indicated in Chapter 3, an interface is the point at which one part of the organisation needs to co-operate and interact with another unit, department, or even division in order to get work done or achieve a particular goal or goals. A straight-line relationship, one based on authority, is easy to respect. The differences in the roles, responsibilities and requirements between two or more parties are relatively clear, as is their area of overlap. A dotted-line relationship is more difficult to manage, as, by the very nature of the relationship, a great deal depends on co-operation and a willingness to work together. The reason for working together may, initially, be unclear, but the benefit of the relationship may emerge as the parties co-operate. Flexibility of response, to customer needs and competitor impact, requires an ever-greater need to respect and act on numerous interfaces inside the organisation. For so many organisations, nurturing interfaces means managing dotted-line relationships. Managing the dotted-line relationships involves getting the best out of that interface without undermining the authority and position of others. Effectively managing interfaces is vital in ensuring positive communication.

Table 4.3 opposite summarises the positive and negative impact of nurturing or neglecting key interfaces in the structure. If one attends to key interfaces, the staff's understanding of how the structure works and who are the key managers in the structure improves. Responsiveness to key relationships enhances personal discipline and information flow, and improves attitudes to work.

Neglecting structural relationships allows certain negative attitudes to grow. Attitudes to change, to internal control mechanisms, and to attending meetings become negative. Personnel in an organisation where the key interfaces in the structure are not respected lose initiative and end up doing only what is required of them. As already indicated, the key to nurturing interfaces is *attitude*. The more positively minded the

Table 4.3 *Making the structure work*

Nurturing the interfaces	Neglecting the interfaces
■ Managers' knowledge of the structure improves ■ Improved discipline ■ Key top managers are known by others ■ Individuals regularly informed on developments ■ Positive attitude to job	■ Inadequate financial controls ■ Poor discipline in attending meetings ■ Confusion when changes take place ■ Negative attitude to change ■ Negative attitude to internal controls ■ People do only what is required of them

senior manager, the greater the likelihood that effort will be applied to ensure the continued effective running of the structure. The more the manager feels isolated or is disenchanted with the system, the more likely he is not to pay attention to making the structure work – he'll just do his job.

Case Study 4.3

FRUSTRATION

A European subsidiary company, embracing the functions of sales, marketing, manufacturing and key support services, in effect, an integrated business entity, of a US hi-tech company, was facing problems with its parent. All of the European directors reported strained relationships with their US counterparts and bosses. The MD, based with his team at the largest of the three manufacturing sites, in Scotland, recognised that circumstances had reached crisis point. In the top team of any subsidiary, certain tensions are likely to exist between one or two directors and their counterparts at corporate headquarters. Such tensions, however, are normal irritants in the running of a business.

In this case, all of the top team members, including the MD, were experiencing severely strained relationships with the US parent, causing disruptive morale problems in the plants. The MD was sufficiently concerned to organise for his team a 'weekend behind closed doors' session, in a country hotel, and invited me to act as facilitator, consultant and helper. We met late Friday afternoon and intended to work until early Sunday evening.

Before dinner on Friday evening, I asked the team to identify and prioritise their current problems and frustrations. They named a number of issues.

■ Reorganisations are too frequent (five times that year) with the result that morale at senior and middle management level is diminishing.

- The sales and marketing focus is not allowed to settle down, as differences of opinion between the US and the European executives and within the US parent itself, as to the sales and marketing practices to adopt, are considerable. The European team stated that, they had a clear and shared view as to the sales and marketing requirements for their products, a view not supported by the US executives.

- The direction and identity of R & D, product development, and customisation seemed to the European team to be dependent on whoever held sway in the US. This whole area was seen as riddled with politics.

- The US executive was introducing new product streams for sales and marketing in Europe, but with minimum consultation and support for the European business.

- Recently, corporate headquarters had changed the spending limits of certain of the UK executives, reduced their budgetary discretion, and strengthened certain dotted-line relationships between the UK, Europe and the US, with the end result that both developments undermined the position of the MD.

For the MD, this last point was the last straw; hence the workshop.

Not knowing the group, I began a process of exploration of their attitudes, level of maturity, team sensitivity, ability to operate in a more sophisticated international structure, and general business acumen, through a series of tests, discussions and exercises, which began late Friday evening and continued for most of Saturday. As the sessions progressed, what clearly emerged was the competency and maturity of each of the directors, and their considerable capacity and still unrealised potential as the top team.

Sunday was spent identifying and exploring approaches for improving and consolidating the relationship with the US corporate bosses.

I was invited to attend a few of the initial meetings with the US executive. Matters did improve somewhat. It was agreed that budgets would not be suddenly changed. The European team would be brought into strategic discussions far earlier than in present practice. Product development, pricing, and marketing would be given more attention in joint discussion and agreement, especially in terms of how particular product streams and channels to market were to be managed.

For the short period after that in which I was involved, events indicated a more positive and cohesive emerging identity between the US parent and its European subsidiary.

Quite by accident, I met the director of manufacturing of the company in Case Study 4.3 a year later and, naturally, I enquired about developments over the past year. 'Well', he said, 'things were going OK for a while and then they went bad. They had a couple of staff changes, and almost overnight they went back to the way they were – not communicating, not discussing, telling us what to do, no support on new product streams and basically treating Mel as an office boy, not as the MD of Europe.' I asked him how the UK team had responded. He replied, 'Now basically as before; we try and do our own thing and take no notice of them!'

Despite constant frustrations, quality of service, product quality and sales were improving. Costs seemed well under control. The continuing poor relationship did not seem to cause any noticeable operational problems. The opportunity costs, however, in terms of penetrating new customer bases are high. This company is, at the moment, doing well with its existing client base. Because of the poor relationships, ever-present strains, and misunderstandings, the European team has lost the will to convince its US bosses that time and money should be invested in increasing market share by extending the customer base.

It is easy to offer, as example of poor practice, a subsidiary of a multinational company operating from the UK as the European headquarters. It is understandable that strained relationships, cultural differences, poor communications, and misunderstandings arise. The same circumstances, however, can arise with a local company in any country. Short-term thinking and restrictive management tend to pay little attention to finding out how to nurture sensitive interfaces in the structure in order to enhance the business. Not that only US companies are at fault. I have witnessed inattentiveness to key linkages in the structure of UK, German, and French parent companies inducing similar opportunity costs in overseas subsidiaries and in divisions and subsidiaries within the respective home countries.

In Case Study 4.3, the subsidiary team was doing its best under strained circumstances. The learning point from this case is not only that it is important to recognise that making the structure work requires effort and application, but also that a negative set of circumstances can continue indefinitely. It is all too easy for the parties involved to become used to the ever-present strains and see them as immovable obstacles. Hence, the situation goes on and on, and the strains become a normal part of everyday life. Bankruptcy is not the danger. It is more that potential remains unfulfilled.

Before entering the field of management development strategy, I worked professionally in psychiatric care and counselling in the community and hospital. Certain of my clients suffered from depressive illnesses, and what struck me was that if they did not want to improve, all that care, counselling and drug therapy could provide was temporary relief. Do you know how long certain people lived with their depression? – a lifetime. With their ups and downs, they existed in their condition, from one day to the next, for the rest of their lives.

The parallel with business organisations may be seen in the casual

chats in the corridor or at lunchtimes concerning the unnecessary frustrations that people manage and somehow overcome on a daily basis.
These frustrations may be dealt with one day but reappear the next, indicating that it is the symptoms, not the problems, that are being addressed.
In certain organisations, a macho attitude emerges,

'I can handle bigger problems than you can'

or

'Do you know how much crap I handled today – more than the rest of the
organisation put together!'

These are probably true statements. My experience of managers who so
comment is that they probably can handle considerable frustrations –
but what wasted effort!

Failure to nurture key interfaces in the structure means that the
structure is unlikely to operate as intended. Even with a professionally
oriented and positively minded management, damaging problems arise.
Uncertainty over budgets and responsibilities and the unnecessary
movement of personnel, demoralise management and staff. Everything
seems to take twice as long to do.

Those with the greatest number of linkages to nurture are the GMs.
Their perception as to how the structure should operate is crucial. The
GMs probably know more than anyone what it really means to run the
organisation – they live it every day. Nurturing the GMs is not only bene-
ficial in promoting key values down the line, but it is also necessary for
the basic running and maintenance of the organisation and its structure.

It is important to recognise that nurturing interfaces is not simply a
concern of organisation structure. Nor is it just a matter of clarifying the
behaviours required in a job description. Nurturing interfaces is a matter
of attitude and communication, in that the senior executives' capacity
for providing direction and example is clearly illustrated by their behaviour
at key interfaces. Those organisations that interface positively have a top
team that has considered what to communicate and especially how to
project the key messages.

I have what we call the top 70, which is the top management team.
We meet from time to time and we have the top 300 grouped from
around the world, where we go away and have a couple of days . . .
That was an experience I found the most uplifting of my life. People

from all over the world communicating our vision and their vision, with feedback over two and a half days.

Tom Frost,
CEO,
National Westminster Bank

Tom Frost's philosophy of support for his management and of working issues through with them is clear in his style of management.

Spreading the message is best done through example – do as I do! This requires personal discipline from each manager consistently to behave in a manner that is appropriate to the requirements of the role and the circumstances, as in Case Study 4.4, below.

Case Study 4.4

THE BOC STORY

BOC, British Oxygen Co., having successfully pursued strategies for growth in the mid-1970s which involved rationalisation, merger with AirCo (in which the CEO, Dick Giordano became the group CEO), reducing costs, upgrading technology, developing new products, and investing in research, is now a world leader in the gas industry. One reason for such success is the management of the organisation.

Giordano, sensitive to the benefits of good communication, has emphasised quality of communication through networking, that is, making contacts and getting to know one another, and one another's problems and constraints. Honesty, trust and openness are key ingredients to effective networking in BOC, and this is due to the recognition that openness without honesty and trust demotivates staff and management alike. Hence, a key value in BOC is *integrity at the interfaces*, namely respect for straight- and dotted-line relationships, an emphasis on horizontal communication, and the nurture of these relationships for the sake of the business. Communication of issues and explanations of decisions and actions are important and necessary behaviours practised by executives in BOC. For example, if the local manager asks for investment commitment to expand a plant, communicating a simple yes or no answer is unacceptable. If the money has been committed elsewhere, then that has to be the true response. Uppermost in the consciousness of senior managers is to ensure that they do not deny the validity of the local managers' plans.

Respect, integrity and responsiveness at interfaces not only improves communication, but also does a 'power of good' to morale.

The philosophy of do as I do requires a recognition from each senior manager that simply behaving as one feels is inappropriate. Being conscious of the impact one makes and the example one sets is crucial to developing a basic set of disciplines necessary for the effective management of the organisation.

BEST PRACTICE INVENTORY

Dos

☐ Identify the key values. What does your organisation stand for? Has any attention been given to identifying the values which provide the background for the mission and identity of the organisation? The survey clearly showed that each organisation has a set of values that fundamentally influence the behaviour of all personnel and hence are central to the management of the structure. Those organisations that have given little consideration to the issue of business values are likely to have a mixture of positive and negative values influencing behaviour. Negative values may not harm the organisation in the short term, but they undoubtedly influence its long-term prosperity and success. Those organisations that have given serious consideration to promoting key business values throughout the business are less likely to be vulnerable in the long term.

☐ Identify what communication means for you and your business! To what extent is the issue of internal communication discussed by the top team? How valuable is such discussion in terms of identifying what communication really means for your organisation? Does communication mean sending more memos? Or does it mean having a more disciplined approach to projecting key messages? Before embarking on any internal communications exercise, identify what is meant by communications. This little exercise in itself will highlight the degree to which internal communications are respected or merely paid lip service.

☐ Write down the mission statement. This assumes that sufficient attention has been given to the mission to enable it to be stated. Identifying the mission provides strong guidelines for the objectives to be set and the key behaviours desired. Once the elements of the mission are identified, write them down as a statement. Consider *how* the mission statement is to be communicated, and *to whom*.

☐ Communicate corporate objectives. In conjunction with the mission statement, clear communication of corporate objectives displays clear direction and that top management are in control. Certainly, discretion needs to be allowed for the communication of functional/departmental, ie local, objectives, but not at the expense of corporate objectives. Crucial is the communication of corporate objectives, which are seen to drive functional/departmental objectives.

☐ Identify those key interfaces in the structure which require nurture. In this way, key issues will be addressed that could otherwise be neglected.

☐ Ensure that a consistent discipline exists within the executive as to the key behaviours of its members. Managers communicate as much by what they do as by what they say. Inconsistent behaviour can, over time, damage the fabric of the organisation, as it causes senior management's ability to lead to be questioned.

Don'ts

☐ Do not be too busy with immediate tasks. Of course, top management work is demanding and considerably time-consuming. However, time has to be made for competently addressing long-term issues, such as strategy and communications, as well as immediate and pressing demands. It is important to reach a balance between completing task activities and addressing the more qualitative issues of management and leadership.

☐ Do not consider that what you face is a time-management problem. If the feeling is that time management is a concern, then it is likely that the real problem is one of role and task allocation. Are you spending too much time on inappropriate activities? Rather than going on a time-management course, perhaps you should reconsider your current practice of delegation. Time management may well be a problem for middle-level managers who have a number of different tasks to complete. For senior management, who have both operational and strategic issues to address, consideration needs to be given to what requires top management's attention and what can be allocated to others. Of course, the issue of trust emerges. If the trust necessary for delegation does not exist, then there may be an underlying communications problem.

☐ Do not assume that words are sufficient. To emphasise the point, just because something has been said or written down, does not mean that effective communication has been achieved. Words have to be accompanied by behaviours, consistent and appropriate for the circumstances.

'Do as I do' is one side of the coin of the skills of influence. The other is being *close to people* in order to gain their ownership of, and commitment to, what you would like them to do. Being close to people is crucial to providing direction and setting good example. It is through intimate understanding of the needs and concerns of others, that managers adjust their behaviour and performance, a flexibility that is necessary in order to address challenges and problems as they arise. Being close to people means that you are *hearing what's said*.

5
Hearing What's Said

Communication is asking other people's advice, listening to what
they have to say, seeking to persuade them.

Rt Hon. Bill Rodgers,
Director General,
Royal Institute of British Architects,
Ex-Secretary of State

Q: *Do you feel feedback is important?*

A: Oh yes, desperately! I wouldn't know how to run it if I did not.
There are people who don't, but it's essential to the way I run
the business. I always say . . . that you are only as good as the
people who work for you.

Gordon Owen,
Group Managing Director, Cable and Wireless,
Chairman, Mercury Communications Ltd

Q: *Who are the real experts concerning the business?*

A: Those staff and management involved in the making, selling and
worrying about the goods and services that are produced by the business.

Q: *Who knows about the customer?*

A: Those staff and management who are dealing with customers and
who are having to address customers' needs and concerns, by both
linking up with the other parts of the business in order to provide
what the customer wants, and then servicing customer needs once
the sale has taken place.

Q: *Who can give top management reliable information on the nature
of the problems the business is facing and what possibly to do next?*

A: Those staff and management further down the organisation who are
dealing with today's and tomorrow's problems.

To run a business consistently well, as stated, involves focusing resources to achieve particular targets. Integrally involved in the processes of achieving goals is the communication of a core set of values that provide identity, meaning and pride in the job to staff and management alike. Part of communication is appreciating just what is happening in the organisation, so that it is possible to gauge the quality of response to the projected goals and values.

The information and raw intelligence required by top management to keep the business on course by adjusting to changing circumstances are available on request. All it takes is to *ask and hear what is said.* Inviting comment and opinion on how effectively the business is being run, what needs to be done to improve present performance, and what obstacles would need to be overcome to improve performance doesn't always induce a thoughtful response. If the everyday intelligence required for running the business is to reach the ears of senior management, planning for a process of feedback must take place.

The advantages to be gained from gathering views on what's happening to the business are considerable. Apart from providing up-to-date information on what is right and wrong with the organisation, information which is invaluable for short-term decision making, and apart from allowing for a natural free flow of opinion to be expressed, such practice displays considerable respect for the real experts in the business – the staff who are doing business daily.

Through talking about the business, managers at various levels have the opportunity to understand each other's problems and constraints, and to help each other to address such needs. Through providing the necessary support and assistance in order to meet the needs of managers at different levels in the organisation, managers allow trust and respect to emerge as key components of the culture of the organisation. Through managers making the time and effort to hear what is said, ownership of the challenges, problems and ways forward becomes an integral part of the business.

Hearing what is said does not involve only polite listening. Hearing what is said requires planning and commitment to devote time to meet and interact with staff and management in the organisation, in order to induce the feeling of comfort necessary for meaningful and open discussion. Relationships need to be nurtured and confidence boosted, for people to state positively and openly what they feel. Hearing what is said involves active listening.

Listening involves three approaches: (1) openness of management style; (2) inviting, receiving and handling feedback well; and (3) managing ambiguity.

OPENNESS OF STYLE

Certain senior managers have been described as open, approachable, and easy to relate to; as persons with whom most issues can be discussed. For bosses, colleagues and subordinates alike, such an orientation is positive and stimulating, for it allows for ease of communication. Does such a positively rated approach occur naturally in certain individuals and not others? No! Any manager can adopt an open style practised in a manner to suit him, as long as he is cognisant of underlying elements of openness. Table 5.1 below highlights the elements of openness.

Table 5.1 *Elements of openness: Results from research*

Element		Purpose
Active encouragement	*to*	Discuss work problems openly
Making time available	*to*	Track progress on key initiatives
Acceptance	*of*	Others' liking/dislike of me
Tolerance	*of*	Differences
Personal discipline	*to*	Practise open style

Active encouragement of colleagues and subordinates to discuss work problems with senior managers is crucial to adopting openness of style. Making it known that you wish to be approached on work problems – for example, by leaving the office door open – has to be coupled with display of a wish to be approached. The attitude a manager projects is a powerful influence on others and their behaviours. If the boss says he wishes to be approached but his behaviour does not seem to indicate so, then it is unlikely that he would be approached unless very serious problems arise.

Not just saying it, but projecting a desire to be approached – how is that done? The senior manager needs to make time available, as by actively tracking progress on key initiatives. Effective practice of openness of style needs to be related to work concerns and an intimacy with the key projects that are under way in the organisation. Tracking progress needs to be a sensitively handled process. The quality of relationship between the senior manager and the others involved needs to be positive, in order to discuss problems that have arisen and why certain projects may not be on target.

In order to induce the basic level of comfort necessary for strengthening relationships, acceptance of others' liking and dislike of you is necessary.

141

Popularity is shallow; respect is long lasting. Furthermore, tolerance of differences, such as differences of personality, or in the way work is done, as long as output is of the necessary standard, allows others to develop their style, their way of doing things. Such tolerance is likely to increase their sense of ownership and identity with their work.

Practising an open style, making oneself available, and working issues through with others in ways they feel comfortable are demanding in terms of time, commitment and emotional energy. It is no surprise to hear managers comment, 'I just don't have the time to go round talking to everyone and listening to them. I really wish I did, but it's just not realistic with the job I've got.' Or, in terms of emotional impact, 'Hearing what others have to say can be draining, especially when you decide not to accept their advice.' It is no surprise to see managers practise more directive styles as their best way of coping with their circumstances.

Considerable personal discipline is required effectively to practise an open style. The discipline relates to control of one's diary in order to make time to hear, as well as to an emotional strength and commitment that may feel like laying oneself open to intertwined comment and criticism. The difference between having and not having the time to adopt a more open style is in the surrounding circumstances, the urgency of commitments made, and the need to develop staff and management. It is true that under certain circumstances there is little time available for the practice of an open style. However, it is worth remembering that the difference between expediency and reality is finely balanced. Adopting a long-term view of a situation and practising a more people-related style which allows for on-the-job development of staff and management, may be feasible but too threatening to practise. The excuse given is that a more open style is really not possible in the short term. If one considers the entire process of making, telling, selling and implementing a decision, it appears likely that more time is lost, by not adopting a more open style as a result of the lack of others' decision ownership.

It is equally not surprising to observe managers who are willing to practise a more open style, but only sparingly. Undoubtedly, the intention is to be open. The comments they receive, however, can induce defensiveness. A *psychological hardiness* is required to tease out helpful insights through negative comments, in order to attain positive outcomes. The ability to accept criticism and not respond defensively emerges from a personal discipline to listen actively.

The survey showed that the practice of openness of style by top management induces, not only in themselves but also in others, high levels of job satisfaction and the ability to manage problems in such a way that they rarely become sources of stress. At worst, difficult problems remain a strain, but they do not become debilitating and stressful. At best, they are resolved.

Openness of style not only keeps one in touch with the rest of the organisation, but also induces in others a greater willingness to address problems.

Case Study 5.1

THE *BELFAST TELEGRAPH*

The *Belfast Telegraph* is a provincial evening newspaper covering Northern Ireland, with lower-volume sales in the Republic of Ireland. The *Telegraph* has regularly served (what is now) Northern Ireland for 120 years, and it is unique in being an evening paper which is also the national newspaper.

Under the leadership of its current MD, Bob Crane, this newspaper has a circulation of 140,000. It has four free daily news-sheets (156,000 circulation), *Ireland's Saturday Night* (a sports paper), and *Sunday Life* (a Sunday paper). The *Belfast Telegraph* is also contracted to print the *Daily Mirror*, the *Sunday Mirror*, the *People*, *Sporting Life*, and *Sporting Life Weekender*, all for the whole of Ireland. The *Belfast Telegraph* is a subsidiary of Thomson Regional Newspapers Ltd, which in turn, is a subsidiary of the Thomson Corporation. The *Belfast Telegraph* is a jewel in the Thomson empire, constantly and positively contributing to the corporate budget.

The *Belfast Telegraph* management and staff work hard. Their equipment is efficient and up to date. Morale is high. Respect and support for Bob Crane is overwhelming.

Bob Crane is a pleasant, quiet man, not the archetypal upfront, dynamic leader, but dynamic in a different way. Everything is done on a team basis. Most of the talking is done by the others. Bob listens. The team and Bob jointly agree what to do and then do it. In that organisation, the consistency and coherence of pushing the same message down the line is admirable. Once the group has decided what to do, should one of the team veer away from what was agreed, he has the other members of the group to face as well as Bob. Feedback is open and free flowing.

Even under the greatest of pressure, Bob makes time for his staff if they want to talk. One of the top team described Bob as the ideal boss, totally concerned with the business and its people.

Despite the pressures of competing in a small market, well stocked with news-sheets and newspapers, and hard work, the staff and management exhibit high levels of job satisfaction, seemingly coping well with pressure and strain.

Bob falls into the category of the positive, listening boss.

Godfrey Golzen, the respected *Sunday Times* business writer, has described Alan Sheppard, the chief executive of the Grand Metropolitan empire, an organisation whose sales currently run at £6bn, as a listening boss who not only is in daily touch with his staff and management, but is also a visionary and driver of the business.

> 'Sheppard says that listening and staying close to customers lies at the heart of visions that work'
>
> Godfrey Golzen (*Sunday Times*, 29 October 1989).

Bob Crane of the *Belfast Telegraph* (Case Study 5.1) falls into the same category. Being heard by your boss with understanding and constructive comment improves not only problem-solving skills but also morale. Staff and management do not feel anxious in talking to the boss about their concerns, as consistent practice of openness is unlikely to bring about the experience of loss of face. With greater openness, far fewer matters are likely to be viewed as inducing loss of face, as people have become accustomed to discussing problems.

By generating well-established channels of communication with one's own people, making visions work and driving the business forward seem to happen naturally.

FEEDBACK

Linked to openness of style is the ability to *invite* feedback. Feedback, through teasing out or being offered information, is crucial to the effective running of a business. Feedback gives staff the knowledge they need to do their work, to achieve standards, and to understand how others are responding to authority and direction. The information that needs to be gathered is both of quantitative, ie what people are doing, and qualitative, ie how they are doing it and feeling about it! In inviting feedback, both elements are required. It is impossible to divorce the giving of information from emotion.

> . . . to come and help me with my own relationships with my colleagues, and in turn that has had a cascade effect. In the past, these things were considered to be wet and slightly embarrassing; you didn't really want to admit that you needed somebody to come and help you to manage change. I made no particular secret of the fact that I was having him [Tom Mannion] go round and interview people saying – 'What do you think of this fellow and what does he do right and what does he do wrong?' It's not a very macho thing to have to admit that you actually don't know how to behave. But it became respectable to use these techniques, and a number of my colleagues started using him to do the same thing for them.
>
> Mark Hely Hutchinson,
> Ex-chief Executive Officer,
> Bank of Ireland

Mark is referring to the Development Support Unit, operating within the Bank of Ireland, which assists managers with their relationships, team performance and the broader business concerns they face in their job. One of the principal tools used by the internal consultants is feedback. Feedback is used to help senior managers understand, come to terms with, and do something about the way they are thinking about, and operating in, the organisation. The information for feedback is gathered from the bosses, colleagues and subordinates of the managers in question. The two key consultants and founders of the Development Support Unit, Tom Mannion and Niall Crotty, are overwhelmed with requests for intervention and assistance. The Development Support Unit is a business within a business. It is a success!

It does help to have professional consultants available to assist and support senior managers with their relationships and in managing change, through using feedback. More often than not, however, such support, either as an internal or an external resource, is not available. It is up to the manager to initiate and manage well the feedback process.

Inviting and receiving *positive feedback* are relatively easy to handle. The manager is being told he is making a positive impact and contribution. Inviting and receiving *both positive and negative feedback* are more sensitive processes. What needs to be said is likely to be perceived as personal and, possibly, hurtful. Feedback may need to be given in order to address sensitive concerns. However, because of the discomfort the dialogue could generate for the parties involved, this feedback is not given. Hence, those concerns remain unspoken.

The blocks to feedback identified in the survey are as follows:

- The senior manager has, to date, in his role and within the structure, not been required to receive feedback and hence his competence to initiate and manage the process is poor.

- The senior manager has never invited feedback, and therefore confidence in others to give feedback is low.

- It may be politically inappropriate to request feedback, as the quality of executive relationships is poor, making it difficult to enter into a deeper dialogue.

- Bosses, subordinates and colleagues have not appreciated the true nature of their problems; they focus on extraneous issues, offer inconsequential feedback, and then become disappointed or even angry when the senior manager cannot or will not act.

- An appreciation of, and sensitivity to, managerial problems in general is low among bosses, colleagues and/or subordinates; hence, there would be little value in requesting and receiving feedback. The survey revealed that such an orientation is particularly prevalent in product-oriented structures where, as shown in Chapter 3, senior managers report that they gain greater satisfaction from the technical/specialist side of their work than from general management, preferring their subordinates to be tidy and well disciplined. To enter into a feedback dialogue in such a working environment could generate considerable resentment or even anger.

- The senior manager may be unaccustomed to, or untrained in, receiving feedback, and hence he bars the offer of information, especially that concerning his performance.

- The senior manager, irrespective of his skills, may be threatened by the nature of the feedback, feel himself unable to cope, and hence fail to initiate a meaningful dialogue.

Case Study 5.2

IT'S SUCH A BLOODY SHAME

A well-known company involved in heavy engineering manufacture had overcome its poor market position and loss of sales by focusing on the needs of particular customer groups and product quality. The company promoted its engineering skills as the key strategy to overcome its difficulties. The strategy worked.

The CEO of the company, a respected and sincere person, felt that the strategy could continue to promote the company to greater success. Discussions at board and internal management team meetings focused on short-term budget forecasts, production efficiencies and costs. The underlying problems of the organisation – such as which other markets to penetrate, how to decentralise the organisation into a greater number of profit centres, the fatiguing working conditions of management and workforce, and the growing militancy of the trade unions, who considered they should have more voice, because of their co-operation in and commitment to improving the company's market position, and their keeping wages at a stable level when the company was in difficulty – were not being discussed. The irritation at not being able to discuss long-term issues with the other executive directors led to their criticising the CEO's leadership style.

On the main board sat non-executive as well as executive directors. To the CEO, the non-execs seemed more helpful and supportive than the executive directors. The CEO began to hold two meetings. Once the full board meeting was completed, he held a separate meeting with his non-executive directors. What was discussed and how formal or informal were the meetings, the executive directors did not know. However, their suspicions deepened. The CEO seemed to confide more and more in the non-execs. The business seemed as if it were being run on two agendas.

Lower down the organisation, relations with the unions and middle-level management grew strained. The effort required to edge into and hold a dominant market position required working considerable overtime, the rates of payment of which failed to satisfy the unions, as did other factors such as working conditions and holidays.

With worsening relationships within the board and with the shop floor, one of the directors attempted a heart-to-heart with the CEO. Although a meeting was arranged between the two, the CEO appeared defensive and really gave his director little opportunity to be frank and open.

The inevitable happened – a strike, right in the middle of servicing a multimillion-pound order. The strike was prolonged. This cash-rich company was cash rich no more. In the opinion of some of the directors, the strike need not have occurred.

In the fifth week of the strike, the board met in an emergency meeting, and voted the CEO off the board, requesting his resignation, which he duly tendered. One of the more mature and aware executive directors commented at the end of the meeting,

'You know, even up to a couple of months ago, all we needed was a weekend away with the boss. We would have told him what we thought about him and the way he was running the company. We also would have told him that he had our full support, which at the time he would have had – it's too late now. All this could have been avoided if he had allowed us to really get together and speak openly. If he only could have got the best out of us. It's such a bloody shame!'

Experience strongly indicates that personal factors, such as not appreciating the true nature of problems, and not appreciating the value of feedback, are the predominant reasons for poor or non-existent conversations about what could be done better. Certainly, the CEO in Case Study 5.2 confided in me after his resignation, kicking his heels at home, that if he were honest with himself, he had understood the problems he was creating; he had recognised that his colleagues, as he put it, 'wanted to have a go at him', and now he wished he had allowed that confrontation to take place.

'When I was younger, I flew planes,' he told me. 'Most of the crashes that I knew of were due to human error. I did just that as a CEO. Theoretically, I knew what the problem was – it actually was up to me and I did nothing about it.'

The message is, a top manager should *leave his ego at home*.

Feedback process

The feedback process involves two considerations. The robustness of relationship that enables feedback to be offered, and the process of giving, receiving and handling feedback.

Robustness of relationship

Certain managers may not exhibit the best people skills, but they are trusted and respected by their colleagues and subordinates. Why?

Others practise effective interpersonal skills, but they are not trusted or even respected. Why?

In order to talk to others openly, offer opinions, and still maintain the conversation without giving offence and generating resentment, it is necessary to have developed a quality of relationship that can cope with openness of conversation. In Chapter 2, one of the abilities attributed to an integrator is that of stimulating a quality of relationship such that feedback can be offered and debated. That quality of relationship is not formed simply through the application of interpersonal skills. Being good at handling people helps, but it is insufficient. It is important to recognise that with certain subordinates, colleagues and supervisors, a more stable and robust relationship is required – a feedback relationship – as openness in talking and offering opinions is necessary for the continuing management of the business.

Identifying who are the managers with whom one requires a more robust relationship is often no problem. In one of my one-to-one counselling sessions with a senior manager from a large manufacturing company, while exploring the lack of team identity among senior executives and the impact of such relationships on the business, my counsellee, with no prompting, identified the problem managers and their effect on other senior managers who were made to feel uncomfortable by certain poor-quality relationships. He also recognised the results of such poor-quality discourse which, to date, had meant poor-quality discussions of strategy. Meetings had focused on operational or more immediately functional concerns. I never once had to ask my counsellee who was part of the problem or what, in fact, were the problems. He knew! I asked how much time he allocated to improving relationships in order to stimulate a climate of purposeful business conversation. The point of that question was to explore the amount of time he allocated to developing relationships to the point where openness of conversation could take place.

No hard-and-fast rules have emerged as to how to spend more time with key colleagues. For my counsellee, walkabout seemed important. He needed to be seen more with his im-mediate subordinates, jointly walking the floor, listening to their more immediate concerns. Other managers organise social events, lunches, dinners, or after-work drinks, in order to break down barriers and generate a more informal atmosphere.

Howard Macdonald, the CEO of County NatWest, the investment banking arm of the NatWest Group, reports that he tries to be at work in the early morning, at times, before 6.30 am, and talks to the traders and others who have to be up for the international markets in transactions of stock and currency. He stays on a bit later than most staff at the end of the day, as other managers in the bank are involved, for example, in the financial restructuring of corporate clients and may meet such clients in the late afternoon or evening. For Howard, it's a long day, but, as the boss, he is always visible, supportive, and in touch. He makes the time to know his people.

Those managers unsure as to how to form key relationships should ask one or two of the staff how to establish a better link. If the question is posed sincerely, and assuming that relationships are not too badly damaged, the questioner will be told one or more of the following:

■ We need to see more of you.

■ Have more and different items on the agenda.

■ Let's have a few social occasions, inviting spouses.

■ We need greater access to you on a one-to-one basis.

■ We need to thrash out our problems by going to a hotel for the weekend and locking ourselves away until everything has been discussed.

Once the decision to allocate time has been made, other managers will clearly indicate how it can best be spent.

Once relationships have been formed – not an easy or straightforward process – discipline should be applied to nurture and maintain them. Three primary rules to nurture and maintain high-quality executive relationships, are identified in the Effective Professional Relationships checklist.

Effective professional relationships: Results from research

■ Recognise need for a *feedback relationship.*

■ Allocate time to form the relationship.

■ Nurture and maintain the relationship.
   – Check with others before acting.
   – Check for views and opinions.
   – Set *ground* rules for giving and receiving feedback.

Check with others before acting
If colleagues are involved with your client, or supplier, or distributor, inform them that you are also involved and discuss with them your

course of action with these external parties. For others to know of your involvement is important in their relationship with the client, since their relationship could be inadvertently damaged. Furthermore, others could offer advice on how to set the relationship on a better footing. On internal issues, checking before acting informs other senior managers as to developments in the organisation. Checking first with others who may be adversely affected by your activities is not wasted effort. Although certain individuals may react adversely, most will appreciate that you have taken time to inform them. Such actions, even on sensitive issues, set the basis for a culture of maturity – managers become issues based – in which personal feelings can be set aside from the discussion of business problems. The practice of checking first saves time! If checking first has become an accepted behaviour, difficult and sensitive problems tend to be addressed and solved without confrontation. Not to check first may involve your finding out later that you have to retrace your steps and start almost from the beginning.

Check for views and opinions

As part of checking first, views and opinions need to be gathered. It may also be necessary to be more proactive and ask for views and opinions on impending issues or actions. Consultation especially helps subordinates to identify with the issues and challenges facing the organisation, so that they can appreciate the nature of the solutions that need to be implemented. Consultation on actions need be undertaken with only a few managers – those directly involved. Consultation on views can be undertaken with many more, namely staff and management; it is as much a mechanism for communication as it is a means for gaining feedback. Furthermore, the process of consistently checking on views increases the levels of maturity of subordinates. Initially, checking on views could be interpreted by others to mean that their views are likely to be implemented. Consultation, for those less mature, could be interpreted as acceptance of their view. Perseverance at this process, coupled with good dialogue between top-, middle- and lower-level management, helps staff and management recognise that they do have channels for upward communication, without necessarily having their views adopted.

Set ground rules

In order to give and receive feedback, what are the ground rules? Has 'permission' been given to give feedback to the boss? Has there been discussion as to how meetings have been managed to date and whether improvement is required? Has there been discussion of process – the way situations, events, meetings and relationships are handled – as well as content – what should be discussed and addressed? From such discourse, certain unspoken ground rules do emerge.

- Say what you like to whom you like at meetings, but cabinet responsibility must prevail after the meeting.

- Explore during the meeting, but do not revisit decisions.

- Tell your colleagues/boss what you want to discuss before the meeting – no surprises.

- If something is not working out, take the time to let others know in order to see what can be done.

One acid test as to whether such an informal set of ground rules operates in your team is to ask colleagues, the boss, or your immediate subordinates what they consider to be the ground rules for business and team discussions. If differing views are offered, the feedback relationship needs further nurture and development.

Giving and receiving feedback

Three steps in managing feedback are offered: (1) invite feedback, (2) receive feedback, (3) handle feedback well.

Invite feedback
Asking bosses, colleagues or subordinates to offer an opinion, especially if the opinion involves commenting on people or, more specifically, commenting on you, is unlikely to produce meaningful words. Requesting feedback with a question such as 'How am I doing?' is likely to elicit the statement, 'Fine – you are doing OK!', a response that means little.

If they are to offer meaningful feedback, others need to be made to feel sufficiently comfortable. As indicated, the relationship between the requester of feedback and the offerers of feedback needs to be nurtured, so that direct and relevant dialogue can occur. Such a relationship, nurtured through working together and simply getting to know one another, allows feedback to become an accepted form of discourse.

Alternatively, the manager may embark on strengthening the relationship by indicating that he wishes to achieve a deeper level of feedback over work performance, quality of relationships, and attitude. In effect, the practice of feedback is the result of an agreed *contract* between two or more people. A Briton, a good friend and client of mine, working for a French company, was offered and accepted a two-year expatriate placement at corporate headquarters in Paris – his first overseas placement. His bosses did not know how to cope with him. He requested feedback on how he was performing from his corporate boss (especially as his surroundings were so new and he had only a short time to make an impact) and was told, 'just fine'. Dissatisfied, he embarked on a process of, in his own terms, 'training his boss' to give meaningful feedback. In his own terms, he is helping his boss to 'behave like a good friend at the dinner table', talking openly and bluntly, instead of 'being very French'. 'It's the only way I will really find out just how I am getting on,' he commented.

Whether the relationship needs developing to the point of being able to talk openly, the levels of maturity of others need to be considered. Asking someone to offer an opinion of you to you requires a basic level of maturity to appreciate why such a dialogue is important, and how to manage the process. Managers unaccustomed to conferring, listening, offering opinion, justifying that opinion, and convincing others through well-reasoned argument are likely to be unwilling to offer feedback. Certain managers rely on the authority in their role to get things done, and have rarely been exposed to the processes of convincing others. Others just 'get on with it' and do recognise the relevance of sitting down and conversing. Managers who lack the maturity to talk to each other are likely to perceive requests for feedback as threatening and possibly respond in a negative or even destructive manner. Hence, before embarking on training your bosses, colleagues or subordinates to give feedback, assess their maturity level. Sometimes, it may not be worth it!

Receive feedback
Structuring circumstances so that feedback can be appropriately given and received is worthy of consideration. Reliance on casual meetings or informal discussions is inappropriate, as certain issues may not be adequately covered, or the more sensitive ones neglected. There is no substitute for organising meetings where issues can be discussed and explored, agreeing, if necessary, to follow up meetings to track progress.

Handle feedback
Well, once the appropriate circumstances have been structured and feedback has been given for exploration to take place and meaningful conclusions to emerge, feedback needs to be handled well by the receiver. As I have already stated, at senior levels it is difficult to divorce issues from personalities, and hence any feedback is likely to generate emotions. In order to minimise the impact any negative emotions may have on the discussion, it is helpful to break down the feedback offered into issues. A potentially sensitive topic, especially at senior levels, is feedback on performance. Such a subject could be reduced to separate issues for conversation.

152

Case Study 5.3

FEEDBACK AND THE GREEKS

The personnel director of Metek, a Greek engineering consultancy company, hired me to run a team-development programme for the top team of the company. The company is interesting. A subsidiary of one of the main Greek banks, this consultancy company was created to provide expert advice to capital projects which are central in the development of the Greek economy. Under the leadership of a highly talented and well-trained Greek engineer, the company grew rapidly. Consultancy advice could be obtained on subjects ranging from information systems to the engineering services of $1 bn industrial plants.

Since the company had made a substantial impact on the Greek economy, the personnel director was of the opinion that the top team needed maturing as executives. In his opinion, the top team was still too individualist and engineering oriented. My first impressions certainly confirmed the individualistic nature of the senior management of the company, but also quick to emerge was their considerable engineering expertise and sharp, intuitive minds. Basically, this was a young and talented team in need of exposure to executive development.

A three-day programme was prepared involving cases, tests and exercises. The group readily identified with the psychometric and management-style tests on the programme. The CEO and his team were being exposed to the processes of giving and receiving feedback. As the three days progressed, it became clear why the feedback issue was so important. This group of talented engineers had started with nothing and within a short period had raised the company to a position of prominence within the Greek market. High-quality skills, advice and care for the client had become accepted as normal practice in the organisation. However, in attempting to provide top-quality client service, the consultant engineers tended to over-identify with their clients, with the end result that they gave some of their time free. For some in the company, it was wrong to overcharge the client. For others, especially the CEO, the problem was not overcharging, but rather a complete undervaluing of the service offered to the Greek market. Whoever was right, pricing differentials existed according to who was leading a project. The inconsistency in quoting and charging for jobs was now noticeable in the market.

The executive-development tests and exercises provided a mechanism for enabling the team members to talk to each other without discomfort. As each of the group members received, shared and discussed various test results, they naturally became acquainted with the processes of giving and receiving feedback. It did not take a great deal of effort to link the test scores with the issues facing the group, especially the inconsistencies on pricing. It would have been impossible to discuss meaningfully this issue without discussing people, as the group members needed to ask each other why one was charging so much for x days' work while another was billing the client for different amounts for projects that theoretically required similar numbers of man days. The personal sensitivities involved had made the members naturally reluctant to confront each other.

> However, on recognising that different persons operate in different ways, hold different values and philosophies, and practise different styles, the group recognised that it was important openly to address issues of personal style and vision in order to mature themselves and their growing business. The group learned that personally sensitive concerns which affect the running of the organisation can be addressed as issues.

The personnel director, Costas Maragos (Case Study 5.3), confided to me after the event that he did not know whether a northern European approach to management development would work within the Greek culture. Experience indicated that this was a shallow concern. The key issue was the openness and enthusiasm of the team to perform well rather than behave according to cultural stereotypes. The CEO, Takis Tzanickos, having successfully developed the consultancy organisation, has with some members of the Metek team, started a new business – Proman – and, as before, is applying his talents to nurture an effective top team. Costas Maragos is now in retailing, adopting a similarly strategic, human resource approach.

The Bank of Ireland provides a parallel.

> I'd done six months before I took over . . . mostly learning by wandering around the organisation and feeling the temperature . . . at the time, I diagnosed a number of things that were urgently needed . . . it was an organisation which was very empire based. There was also a lot of territorial warfare going on. In particular, there were two main divisions of the bank . . . with a lot of highly unproductive battling between them, even to the extent that it was felt worse to lose business to the other division than it would be to lose it to a competitor.
>
> Q. What did you do?
>
> I tried to create an organisation which had as its principal objective to generate a collegiate style. It was based on something I had done in my previous job in similar circumstances. This was to create a row of executives with no clear divisions you could decipher. We had about twenty responsibilities to parcel out among five or six of us. They were parcelled out in a fashion that had no obvious pattern. Just about every decision had to be taken by one or two people in conjunction with each other. For example, somebody might have the responsibility for branch banking, but somebody else would have the responsibility for personnel, so you couldn't actually do much in the branch banking area without consulting the person who was responsible for personnel . . . so on every decision, at least two people were going to be involved. I saw it as a temporary thing

which we would do to get the team working together; after a bit they would start getting frustrated about it and they would want to change.

It was a slightly strange arrangement but I think it worked well for a period. Inevitably, it had a limited life and we had to change to a more conventional divisional structure in 1988. But the collegiate style that we developed there has survived the delegated divisional structure that we've had for the last couple of years. There is a high level of give and take when we get together to decide cross-divisional issues, with everybody willing to accept whatever is in the group interest. There is a high degree of acceptance that the group interest must precede the divisional bottom line.

Mark Hely Hutchinson,
Ex-chief Executive Officer,
Bank of Ireland

Once person-oriented concerns are viewed as issues, the emotive sting tends to be taken out of the discussion and so encourages further examination.

Having made such a contribution to the Bank of Ireland, Mark Hely Hutchinson unexpectedly resigned in November 1990. Although the bank was initially shocked, a quiet confidence quickly emerged. The overall opinion was that he had so strengthened the bank that it could now stand on its own feet. Unfortunately, the economic conditions in the US and the UK resulted in losses for the two overseas subsidiaries, leading to a substantial fall in profits for the group in the first half of 1990. The bank, however, maintained profitability as it had maintained its position in the domestic Irish market. From the measures that had been and are being introduced in the New Hampshire and the UK operations, it is highly likely that once the current negative economic conditions subside, the bank will re-establish its expected level of profitability. Regrettably, the level of support and opportunity for development afforded by this man to others and to the overall organisation was not reciprocally given to him through this temporary downturn in the Bank of Ireland's performance.

MANAGING AMBIGUITY

Where no clear solution can be applied to an organisational or strategic problem; where senior managers, at times, adopt positions which undermine or contradict each other; or where the straight- and dotted-line relationships in the structure, at times, cause confusion, but for various reasons little seems to be done to alleviate the situation, the managers running the business are facing a situation of ambiguity.

Under circumstances of ambiguity, the potential for miscommunication and misinterpretation is high. Controlling outcomes is difficult, for much depends on the skills of persuasion and understanding, as command and direction are unlikely to be effective. Not so much through bloody-mindedness, as because of the problems they face in their role which limit their manoeuvrability, managers may find themselves in conflict with colleagues, and unable fully to identify the cause of the problem themselves, and hence unable fully to pursue corporate goals. Situations of ambiguity and contradiction require a more understanding approach – a listening style – as, until the nature of the problems facing each senior manager and the options available to him are appreciated, it is unlikely that a realistic pathway forward will be identified.

Circumstances of ambiguity and lack of clarity tempt managers to adopt a 'let's get in there and sort it out' approach, on the assumption that a manager with strong character cuts through the mess. However, devoting time to appreciate the problems, recognising that the deep-seated nature of the problems affords no easy solution, and then adopting a more sensitive style are likely to win over staff and management. Organisational and strategic ambiguity is a phase that needs to be worked through, and that simply takes time.

Case Study 5.4

ROYAL INSTITUTE OF BRITISH ARCHITECTS (RIBA)

A most interesting organisation, certainly not large but undoubtedly not easy to manage, largely because both the nature of the work and the purpose of the RIBA are to service the current and future needs of a body of professionals – architects. What should the role, shape and identity be of a professional organisation which is determined to influence the architectural debate in the UK and yet at the same time be sufficiently pragmatic to collect members' dues, upon which the institute depends? Although it is a professional association, its financial structures strongly imply that the RIBA is a business.

The appointment in 1987 of Bill Rodgers to the post of director general of the institute has had a fundamental impact on the organisation. Bill Rodgers, ex-Parliamentarian, a former Labour secretary of state, and a founder member of the SDP (Gang of Four), was turning his hand to professional management. He recalls:

> So the first thing, the staff were demoralised, there was no sense of direct control or management . . . The second problem was the one that I most

immediately perceived and tried to remedy . . . an area which became a no-man's-land, with all the hazards involved, between elected members who were ultimately responsible for policy decisions, and management, and given that the management wasn't clear-headed or forceful enough, increasingly the elected members began to try to assume a management role. I don't think there is any doubt now about what members can do and what I can do . . . But the immediate problem was financial . . . there was a total absence of financial control.

At the time, the institute, with a turnover of £5m, had a budget deficit of £1.3m. Bill Rodgers continues:

Because we depend on membership subscriptions which are all due at the beginning of the calendar year, we were discovering that very substantial sums of money were lying in Post Office bags on the floor until somebody had found time to take them out, check them and bank them.

With these frustrations and a recognition in the institute of the need for change (Bill considers his appointment was the product of that recognition of the need for change), Bill set about managing change through people. *'I . . . decided to . . . get more of the staff to perform better.'*

Bill emphasised that the reporting relationships required a more professional attitude and approach to meetings. He improved communications with the governing body, the councils, and members. Also, he introduced training, brought in consultants, addressed the financial issue, and has constantly striven for improved understanding among staff and management of the workings and contribution of each of the departments of the institute. The RIBA today is visibly much more professional and responsive to client and colleague needs. Bill says, *'I will be remembered . . . for much better financial management, much better personnel management. I can leave behind a clearly defined culture.'*

On this basis, improving the regional structure of the RIBA and developing the architectural library, probably the finest architectural library in the country, into one of the finest in the world are now strong possibilities.

For all the changes Bill Rodgers introduced and supported (Case Study 5.4), an essential element of his strategy was to establish a respect for performance, both professional and managerial. Bill intended, and is achieving, a cascade effect by providing example from the top. By attending to issues of structure; by being sensitive to and carefully nurturing key interfaces, especially by being aware of the concerns of staff and external members; by understanding the nature of the blockages to communication; and by displaying a capacity for tolerating, managing, and even utilising ambiguity, Bill has brought about positive results. The unusual position of the RIBA, being somewhere between a trade association, a debating society for architectural practice and philosophy, and a trade union, indicates that ambiguity will always be present, but need not be damaging.

BEST PRACTICE INVENTORY

Dos

- ☐ Adopt an open style, especially if you wish to make a long-term impact on the organisation. An open style allows improved communication and a better appreciation of the problems, concerns and challenges of staff and management lower down the organisation. It is often stated that adopting an open style does not provide sufficient focus (meaning it's too soft). Experience shows the reverse, for considerable self-discipline is required effectively to utilise an open style. It is also often stated that too much time is taken up in practising an open style. Certainly, adopting such a style is time-consuming; hence, a choice must be made between time for attention to immediate demands and time to stimulate feedback and thereby a more accepted leadership style.

- ☐ Work on developing robustness of relationships. Necessary for feedback to take place is the recognition of the need for a feedback relationship. Time needs to be taken to develop particular relationships so that important conversations can take place. Nothing special needs to be done to develop such robustness, other than being considerate to bosses, colleagues and subordinates in daily work, especially checking with them before acting on important matters.

- ☐ Think feedback. It is necessary to invite, receive and handle feedback well. By working towards a robustness of relationship and by adopting a style suitable to the feedback process, most of the blockages to feedback can be overcome.

- ☐ Come to terms with ambiguity. In today's mid-to-large-sized corporates, it is unlikely that relationships and interlinkages will be straightforward. Managing incompatible demands requires a tolerance for ambiguity, as solutions may not easily emerge.

Don'ts

- ☐ Do not expect relationships to improve and a feedback culture to emerge quickly. Establishment of a positive dialogue does not occur overnight. Stimulating positive relationships requires time, no matter how sensitive and skilful the manager. The trick is to recognise how long it would take to change attitudes and to induce a more positive environment with the key managers in question.

One underlying theme in this chapter is maturity. The ability to invite, receive and handle feedback well; the discipline required to practise a more open, listening style; and the patience and tolerance to work through ambiguous and unclear issues and circumstances while maintaining cohesion and improving morale among staff and management; these are the elements of executive maturity.

Maturity, which is prerequisite to nurturing interfaces, effectively working the dotted- and straight-line relationships, and stimulating cohesion and consistency in the senior executive with the intention that good practice be cascaded down, is a crucial personal quality in the attainment of business success. Maturity is required calmly to recognise the nature of the problems facing the manager and the necessary steps to take to address them. The emotionally mature manager is likely to be pragmatic, conscious of the time required to work through a change programme, and sensitive to knowing what is required to change attitudes and behaviour. The mature manager is able to consider the nature of problems without alarming emotions, such as anger and anxiety, or undue haste clouding judgement. Maturity, listening, and effective teamwork go hand in hand.

Improving the level of maturity of senior and middle managers through greater self-understanding and deeper insights into economics, market behaviour and society is fundamental in strategies for *sustaining momentum!*

PART III
SUSTAINING
MOMENTUM

We believe there are very substantial economies to be reaped from getting it right the first time.

Dr Tony O'Reilly,
Chairman, President and CEO,
HJ Heinz Co

6
Success Culture

We established five key things that we wanted to do in the company some years back. Firstly, it was to be a marketing company . . . we felt in need of some differentiation in the face of competition . . . The second thing we wanted to establish was that we had to be fair to our employees at all levels, we had to treat people better than our competitors . . . The third thing we wanted to achieve was low-cost producing – this is easy to say, lots of people endeavour to do it, we think we have achieved that. The fourth thing that we wanted to achieve was a company that had a unique *esprit de corps* . . . Fifth . . . we developed a very high pride in our people.

Dr Michael W J Smurfit,
Chairman and CEO,
Jefferson Smurfit Group plc

John Jefferson Smurfit, a master tailor of St Helens, Lancashire, married into the McGee family of Belfast, who 'had a broken-down box business' he founded and, with his sons, developed a multinational that has outgrown its Irish roots. The Smurfit group has become a leader in the paper and board business. The group reported, in 1989, a turnover of IR£1.37bn with pretax profits of IR£236m. The two extraordinary deal makers, Michael Smurfit, a son of John Jefferson Smurfit, and Howard E Kilroy, president and chief operating officer of the Smurfits group, spent the 1980s buying US companies in the industry; they then merged the US operations into a new company, and remortgaged it, leaving 50 per cent interest in the parent company and the sum of £1bn, which is to be used for further acquisitions. By any measure, the Smurfit story is one of outstanding achievement. It is a story of success from humble roots.

The Smurfit formula is clear: effective marketing, low-cost production, and a sensitive handling of, and focus on, personnel and customers.

That is one formula.

> Added value is, by definition, not objective but subjective. It is, for
> that reason, elusive and fearsomely difficult to quantify. It is a quality –
> and qualities are often impossible to measure.
>
> Martin Sorrell,
> CEO, WPP Group plc,
> Speech to the Cranfield Management Association,
> 21 November 1989

Depending on the circumstances and the history of the organisation and
whether it has experienced organic and/or acquisition based growth,
determining success varies according to situation.

> The key success factor in terms of my period of stewardship is
> whether we can make the change away from a product-based
> organisation to a relationship-based organisation . . . The problem
> is quite simply that the majority of the senior executive ranks, and
> by that I mean the Partners and the bands immediately below Partners,
> have spent a long time operating as project-oriented people. They
> are unsure of their ability to operate in a relationship management
> fashion, and because they are unsure and because it demands a signifi-
> cant behavioural change, they are not very keen on doing it if they
> don't have to . . . I want them to place the client at the centre of all
> our business activity.
>
> Colin Sharman,
> Senior South East Regional Partner,
> KPMG Peat Marwick McLintock

In contrast, for Colin Sharman, changing the strategic focus of the business
and adapting the structure to support the strategy, are dependent on
changing the attitudes and behaviours of senior staff and management
of KPMG Peat Marwick. For KPMG Peat Marwick, attitudes are the most
important concern.

Each organisation tells its own story. There are no secrets to success!
For mid-to-large-sized corporates, sustaining momentum is partly
dependent on the creation of a *success culture* within the organisation;
but also partly on recognising what damage can occur if the methods
outlined in the previous chapters are not effectively practised in order to
prevent problems before they arise.

A CULTURE THAT BREEDS SUCCESS

Through an apt combination of shaping skills and influencing skills, and
depending on the application of such skills by the members of the senior
executive, a set of attitudes and basic behaviour patterns begins to

emerge at all levels of staff and management. Such a pattern of thinking, feeling and doing is known as a *culture*. The longer a particular pattern is practised and pursued, the deeper rooted is the culture, the more difficult the culture is to change, and the greater is the time required to raise the level of awareness at senior- and middle-management levels as to the shape and impact of the current culture.

No organisation has only one culture. A number of cultures operate concurrently, depending on the shape of the structure, on the region, on product/service streams, or on whether decision making is centralised or decentralised. The predominant attitudes may be positive, for example, success oriented. Alternatively, the predominant attitudes and behaviours may be more negative, depending on the history of the organisation and the standards set by top management. As has been emphasised in this text, a number of organisations exhibit attitudes and behaviours that are not conducive to success, such as not responding to client needs, not sufficiently nurturing customer bases, and being too internally focused.

However, establishing a culture in which there is 'confidence to act' and in which 'quality of service and people count' is an element that underlies successful businesses.

Confidence to act

Staff and management need to feel a confidence that their actions will be supported by top management. Both are pursuing activities in the best interests of the business.

> We like to delegate and leave people as free as possible, so we try to push management decisions down the line. We run Rolls Royce with a very thin corporate structure.'
>
> Lord Tombs of Brailes,
> Chairman, Rolls Royce plc

For middle- and lower-level management and staff to have the confidence to act, they must have confidence in senior management's capacity and acumen to allow for greater discretion of decision making and action. For senior managers to develop a culture of delegation, they must have confidence in their middle and lower management's ability to perform as assigned and to meet objectives.

Trust in lower-level management to respond positively to greater responsibility is dependent on two factors, both requiring to be initiated by senior management.

165

Being an 'in touch' management

Being an 'in touch' management, ie one aware of external issues concerning clients, suppliers and distributors, as well as of internal issues such as management and staff's response to client needs, the nature of the frustrations and blockages in the structure, and what stimuli lead to improved performance, is considerably facilitated by a culture of *upward communication*. Through consistent communication, senior management are permanently aware of issues and developments.

As indicated in Chapter 5, there is no secret to feedback, other than to ask for views and information, and behave in ways which emphasise an interest and concern for relevant feedback. Overall, do top management behave in such a manner? Middle and lower-level managers were asked to rate their bosses. Sixty-five per cent of respondents view chairmen, CEOs, MDs and directors as effective business leaders who provide direction and the necessary focus to meet targets. The GMs, however, are seen as being the integrators within the organisation (58 per cent of responses). In terms of personal style, 58 per cent of chairmen, CEOs and MDs are perceived as cautious. GMs, however, are perceived as being more open than chairmen and CEOs.

The results indicate a cautious perception that openness and respecting the process of integrating personnel with the organisation for the effective running of the business still require attention. The problems of variation of style, as seen in top managers who send 'mixed messages down the line', are recognised. Top management is perceived as distant; it is felt that directors irritatingly leave the more sensitive aspects of people management to the next level below. For Gordon Owen, Group managing director of Cable and Wireless, this is poor-quality management,

> I get a lot of feedback from further down . . . I have extremely good relations with a lot of people in Cable and Wireless who aren't direct reports to me now, a lot of my colleagues whom I joined the Company with are one or two levels down, with whom I never stopped being friends. In a professional way, I can get them talking to me about things, protecting their anonymity, so it helps me in the management situation.

Taking the time for upward communication occurs when top managers recognise the benefits of such practice. Through being aware of issues as they arise, managers do not allow problems to deteriorate to the point of becoming major concerns. The process of upward communication, for staff and management, is in itself a motivator. Top managers need to show they care and are taking the time to listen. In Chapter 5, we explored the giving and receiving of feedback as an individual skill. Sustaining an environment where upward communication becomes a norm requires additional attention.

An upward-communication culture can be achieved through the following steps:

1. Practise the giving and receiving of feedback within the top team.
    (a) Do directors give their boss feedback? How often?
    (b) Who, genuinely, has enquired whether the GMs feel comfortable in their dialogue with the directors, and whether the feedback given covers the 'total picture'?
    (c) Do members of the top team give each other feedback on issues concerning each other's contribution to the team, personal style, and delivering on commitments made, or on how another person's running of his function is affecting other departments or functions?
    (d) Are there still sensitive issues that are left unstated or that are discussed informally, outside the constituted meetings, indicating that key issues involving both people and the business remain unaddressed?

(If the answers to these questions are more negative than positive, then consideration should be given to establishing a culture of feedback within the top team, as a first step to improving communications in the organisation.)

2. Establish a practice of upward communication through the line. Upward communication should be encouraged through the managerial hierarchy so that all levels of management become accustomed to listening and responding to the concerns and challenges of their subordinates. Being an in-touch management should involve the whole of the management and not just the senior levels. If top managers are serious in stimulating an upward communication culture, then they need to be aware of which levels of management may not respond positively to such an initiative. In order to overcome such resistance, a strategy of training and development needs to be introduced to help managers cope with the changes of behaviour required in their roles.

3. Promote the appraisal process. Appraisal is a fundamental process in establishing a work-related dialogue between bosses and subordinates with a view to improving performance through feedback. The appraisal of subordinates should be a two-way process, whereby the subordinate explains to the boss what additional support is required and what problems or irritations need to be addressed in their relation-

ship, in order to stimulate improved levels of performance. All levels of management need to be encouraged to take appraisal seriously.

4. Organise lunches, dinners, and informal meetings as a forum where senior managers can meet middle- and lower-level managers. In effect, keep in touch by inviting a select number of managers spend time talking about internal and external issues in a more relaxed environment, but in circumstances where they have to talk. Similarly, encourage line managers to organise lunches, dinners and more informal gatherings with their own staff, so that they, too, are better informed when meeting with top management.

5. Go walkabout, as a regular and disciplined practice of visiting regional offices, subsidiary locations, and, with the full knowledge of line management, clients, in order to learn about and experience the standards of service offered.

6. Go on away-days or away-weekends of the sort in which top managers retreat to a country hotel to discuss, in depth, current concerns and future practice and direction. Apart from being more isolated from the disturbances of the office, the away-day practice accustoms senior managers to talk to each other more openly.

7. Encourage feedback on key behaviours. What key behaviours are necessary in order to do the job; are they recognised; and if they are, do colleagues counsel each other as to how to improve their behaviours?

Freedom to act

The 'in touch' senior managers, aware of the strengths and weaknesses of the organisation, the opportunities that can be addressed, and the development needs of the business, can recognise what latitude to give managers down the line to enable them to act as required by their circumstances. Delegating down the line involves the following points:

- Treating mistakes as a part of learning. A fine line exists between responding to mistakes made as a part of the learning process, and allowing a situation to deteriorate through poor discipline and control. A great deal is dependent on the ability of the boss and subordinate to create an environment for discussion, so that both learn to prevent similar circumstances from arising.

- Establishing an appropriate balance between the *accountabilities and responsibilities* in key roles.

- Allowing for feedback up the line.

- Senior managers viewing as an integral element of their job clear communication of corporate objectives.

In response to the question, *'In your current role, what areas/objectives are you pursuing?'*, senior managers gave the following responses:*

Communicating corporate objectives	21 % of responses
Team building	22 % of responses
Training and development	23 % of responses

* Percentage of total responses.

The survey results highlight the emphasis placed on the communication of objectives, and the development of people.

QUALITY OF SERVICE

High-quality performance is fundamental to the generation of a success culture. A quality of performance leading to high levels of quality of service requires organisation and planning.

Addressing the culture

The first step to service quality is to examine the predominantly held attitudes inside the business.

> You will never achieve quality externally until you have quality internally. It's the way you treat each other internally which will eventually lead to how the engineer, when he carries that tool bag on site, treats the customer.
>
> Ken Cusack,
> MD, Sorbus UK

It is crucial to ensure that neither managers nor functional areas within the company become insular. Hence, targeting on individual performance needs to be accompanied by rewards based on overall company performance. There has to be a push from the top constantly to focus people on the business as a whole, a process which demands that top managers respect, make the time for, and clearly explain how they will practise communication. Through educating on the job and making staff and management aware of the issues affecting the company overall, the need for relating to each other across departments, and not being territorially driven, becomes apparent.

* Percentage of total responses.

> We are internal customers to each other. We have to feed from each other and work with each other all the time . . . For example, you cannot answer the phone in two ways, one if it is internal and one if it is external. You answer the phone in one way and that is a quality way.
>
> Ken Cusack

Documenting quality of service

To drive the concept of quality of service effectively throughout the organisation, quality of service needs to be documented. A properly documented policy shows the degree to which the organisation is serious about performance improvement and in which areas. The key tasks and activities that need attention, the internal and external interfaces that need nurture and care, and the fundamental behaviours that staff and management need to adopt should be written down, highlighting those areas where measurement of performance will take place.

Sorbus, being a computer maintenance company, needs to be sensitive to the time it takes to respond to clients, because if the client's mainframe computer goes down, chaos emerges. If the central computer of a customer breaks down, it is of vital concern when the maintenance engineers can arrive. Sorbus produces league tables, not only of performance achieved, but also of key indicators in terms of quality. One of their league tables addresses the issue of response times: response times to clients and what sort of clients – new or well-established – even response times in terms of the speed with which telephone calls are answered and logged are tabulated. Such information is distributed to staff and management. Sorbus' emphasis on quality has led the company to be registered as BS (British Standard) 5750. Ken Cusack says, 'Service is all we do. We've got no captive or niche markets. If we don't perform and do it well, we lose the business. It's as simple as that.'

Driven from the top

The push for quality improvement must be consistent and driven from the top. No one can be exempt! In fact, any programme for improving quality of service highlights existing deficiencies which need attention, often requiring personnel to make substantial, not just cosmetic, changes. If top managers especially are not seen to be making changes in their own practice and behaviour in line with the requirements of the programme, it is likely that the initiative will collapse.

> By establishing quality down the line, we rid ourselves of years of accumulated bureaucracy, and establish efficient, effective, durable

procedures. Needless to say, we made it clear that these measures were not suggestions. You didn't take it or leave it, as you saw fit: you took it.

Now the benefits are beginning to show, and we have got our market share back. When we started this scheme in 1983, we showed £150m profit. In '84, '85, and '86, profit remained at around 165m. By '87, it was up to £240m and reached £360m in 1988.

And just to remind you, we achieved this by making quality flow through line management, and by driving home the concept of customers inside and outside the organisation.

Sir Derek Hornby,
Ex-chairman, Rank Xerox, UK
Excerpt from the summary of an address given at an Odgers lunch
for chief executives.*

The Bank of Ireland was accorded the Quality Mark in 1989 by the Irish Quality Association (see Chapter 4), the bank being the first Irish financial institution to receive it. To win this award, the bank underwent a demanding assessment process designed to establish whether its level of quality practice was sufficiently high to merit full assessment. One of the key criteria was, 'proof of active executive commitment, participation and leadership'.

Heinz has a programme termed TQM – total quality management.

We believe there are very substantial economies to be reaped from getting it right the first time. That involves setting targets that define what you mean by getting it right the first time, and also having accounting computational advisers who are able to compute whether you are in fact improving margins by certain procedures. The second thing that we are concerned with, is that the consumer is getting increasingly concerned about diet and nutrition, calorie counting and body watching . . . so pesticides, fungicides, insecticides are very germane to calculations and costs of auditing procedures . . . The final thing . . . is that we have the vehicle of *Weight Watchers*, which is the premier vehicle in the world, and there are probably going to be something like 70 million individual attendances at our classes in the world. These classes represent both an income source in themselves and also a major opportunity to tell people that they should go and buy weight watchers' food in the local grocery.

Dr Tony O'Reilly,
Chairman, President and CEO,
HJ Heinz Co

* For further details, see Odgers, Executive Search Consultants, Issue no 13.

From Heinz and the innovative weight watchers' concept, to Rank Xerox, to the Bank of Ireland, communication of the policy is coupled with active participation and enthusiastic implementation of quality by top management.

'People count'

The message that 'people count'; that the care and development of personnel is an integral element of the mission of the organisation, is dependent on the behaviours adopted by top management. Managing people in a manner conducive to the growth of the business and the development of individuals involves the practice of two basic disciplines.

Discipline to communicate and listen

The term *communication* has been used on a number of occasions in this book. As stated in Chapter 4, the practice of issuing news-sheets and newsletters and organising briefing groups is helpful. Fundamental, however, are identifying and facilitating those key behaviours which senior managers need in order to *project a positive and motivating image* to the rest of the organisation. Senior managers need, then, to educate middle and junior levels of management in the same behaviours. The following questions are relevant:

- Do managers know what key behaviours support delegation, quality of service and attention to people?

- Do managers make time to spend with staff?

- Do managers work towards establishing ownership of the policies and objectives of the organisation?

To build and develop individuals and groups into high-performing work teams requires the discipline to care about people and to identify and facilitate key behaviours.

Discipline in meetings

Meetings are a key forum where the current and future issues affecting the organisation are addressed. The fundamentals of an organisation are debated, actions are identified, and the commitment to pursue activities is gained. These processes are addressed at meetings. For a meeting to function effectively, its members need to respect that forum. In order to respect meetings, two factors need to be considered – the purpose of the meeting and the skill of running meetings.

In your organisation, are meetings

■ for information giving;

■ a discussion forum;

■ for decision making (operational);

■ for decision making (strategic);

■ simply obligatory to attend?

Do the participants in the key meetings held in the organisation agree on why they are attending the meeting and what their contribution is to be? The greatest frustration occurs when the purpose of the meeting is not clearly understood. Staff can live with the fact that they may not agree with the purpose of meetings, but not to know what is expected of them at meetings is tantamount to asking staff deliberately to waste time. It should be remembered that the vast majority of people go to work with the intention of positively contributing. Exceptionally few start their working day by intending to perform poorly or destructively. The way certain organisations are managed, however, especially the way meetings are run, may result in a number of individuals feeling negative by the end of the day.

Most senior managers pay attention to job roles, attempting to ensure that the tasks, accountabilities and responsibilities are relatively, clearly structured, so that staff and management know what is expected of them, how their performance is to be assessed, and what they are being paid for. Hence, why not pay the same attention to meetings? After all, meetings are the mechanism for groups to inform each other as to developments, identify actions and objectives and offer commitment to implement those actions.

Once the purpose of the meeting has been decided, a basic discipline of attending meetings needs to be introduced. For Bill Rodgers, director general of the RIBA, only illness excuses the attendance of senior managers at the Monday morning executive meetings. Even though most of the time at the meeting is spent on giving information, at least the executive of the RIBA is provided with up-to-date information and the latest views on issues, which are important in helping each senior manager respond to queries. Furthermore, the discipline of attending meetings strengthens the identity of the senior team. The senior group behaves as a positive team. The team members interact in a supportive manner. The team members realise when a colleague requires support and respond accordingly.

The skills of running and effectively interacting in meetings need to be given attention. The skills required for running meetings, in theory, are simplicity itself. They include:

- Listening to the contribution of others.

- Not interrupting, when others are speaking. Each team member and not just the chairman, should make his colleagues aware of such behaviours in order to ensure clarity of communication.

- *Clarifying meanings* by periodically asking others at the meeting for their understanding of the issues discussed and the points made and agreed to, so as to ensure full appreciation of the topics in question.

- Ensuring *involvement and contribution* by all those present, by inviting comment or asking for reactions to comments made by others, and especially drawing in the quieter members of the group.

The practice of these simple guidelines can substantially improve the quality of discussions and the effectiveness of meetings, in terms of addressing the agenda items within the time allowed.

DAMAGE

Shaping the future, the team, and the structure to accommodate the mission and objectives; focusing and motivating staff and management to pursue particular targets; communicating with them clearly and allowing for upward feedback so as to stimulate an environment where ownership of the policies of the company and a confidence and a willingness to succeed predominate; these are the elements of successful performance at the individual and team level identified in the top-executive survey.

There is no secret to success! Success, specifically, means something different to each different organisation. However, we have identified a *recipe for failure*.

The work of top management should be primarily concerned with strategy, long-term trends, policy, and the implications of strategic choice. If the senior executives of an organisation concentrate too much on operational issues and details, the organisation is likely to be seriously at risk over the long term. Hence, senior managers need to pay as much attention to strategic as to operational issues. Errors that occur are as likely to be errors of judgement as operational mistakes. Mistakes are likely to show quickly as mistakes. Mistakes are likely to induce operational costs. Once an operational cost (mistake) is realised, remedial action can be taken.

Errors of judgement are unlikely to show themselves in the near future. Inappropriate decisions made now are unlikely to be realised until considerable time has elapsed. At times, it may even not be clear that the problems of today are the result of poor decision making in the past. Although errors of judgement are unlikely to be realised immediately they do lead to either a slow deterioration of performance, or an inability to pursue all likely avenues of success. In effect, errors of judgement induce *opportunity costs* (See Chapter 2 for more on opportunity costs).

Sources of the damage

Seven areas of opportunity cost are identified.

Inappropriate allocation of overhead

Structuring an organisation to achieve particular objectives involves focusing people and resources to operate in markets, geographic regions, or sectors of the community. Focusing effort through the structure assumes that the senior team has appreciated and discussed current market, regional or community conditions, and shares a reasonably clear understanding as to future trends.

What, however, if such understanding and assumptions about the future are inaccurate or poorly discussed, or if disagreement still exists as to what sales and marketing mean for the business? Organisation structures identifying line functions and support functions may be created, yet they may not be clearly focused on achieving objectives. In fact, a considerable level of overhead may be put in place, in terms of personnel, units or departments, which is intended to generate business, but cannot fully do so because of mistaken assumptions concerning market conditions. Those functions or departments may not have control of all of the resources they need, or may have to interface inappropriately with another part of the organisation. Such interactions may lead to irritations and poor-quality executive relationships, leading, in turn, to limited co-operation and sharing of resources between departments. What may seem to be a problem between people may have, as its roots, a problem of organisation structure. In order to compensate for such blockages, one department may increase its level of costs by hiring the personnel or services that it would otherwise have requested from other functions or departments.

Splits in the top team, unclear thinking concerning the processes of sales and marketing, and sheer ignorance may lead the top team to establish a weighty infrastructure in the hope of generating considerable business activity, instead of organising a small, more robust and more focused organisation to explore or penetrate a particular market. Unclear assumptions about the structure lead to a weak business push. Being kept busy, involvement in considerable activities, and a feeling of constantly handling mini crises, accompanied by poor profitability, can become the norm. Activity, not added value, becomes the accepted practice. Turnover, not profitability, becomes the pursued objective.

Not addressing competitor impact

Poor-quality interactions among the members of the top team are likely to lead to poor quality discussions about the business. Furthermore, if top managers do not fully discuss business developments, then staff and management lower down the structure are unlikely to be encouraged to discuss market and economic circumstances. As a result, the management of the organisation could become too internally focused, and the key issue of the impact competitors are likely to have on the business may be neglected.

Any quantifiable data on market trends and competitor behaviour are of value, but are not necessarily a prime inspiration to act. Such data can go out of date relatively quickly, and take considerable time to gather, process, validate and present. In the meantime, the world has moved on! Furthermore, even if the market-based data are not out of date, managers may not have the maturity, capacity or even interest to identify with the data. Indeed, certain organisations seem to make much use of consultants, projects and surveys, but rarely utilise the information they are given – a situation of analysis-paralysis.

Meaningful debates concerning competitor behaviour are of a qualitative nature; these are discussions which should take place naturally and almost daily. Essentially, they are an expression of each manager's perceptions as to which competitors are doing what; why; and what the impact will be on the organisation. Ideally, quantitative data should be combined with qualitative views in order to stay ahead of the competition.

> With a 'me-too' product, what the hell can you do? – everyone's a low-cost producer, but to become a genuine low-cost producer, to achieve that, we have probably the biggest data bank of any of our competitors. We know much more about them than they know about us . . . Over years and years and years, I bought one share in nearly every paper company in the world, much to their annoyance, because they had to send me annual reports, posted for one share. I did it 15 or 20 years ago. Knowledge was power and I had knowledge!
>
> Dr Michael Smurfit,
> Chairman and CEO,
> Jefferson Smurfit Group plc

The sum of the perceptions of the members of the top team, sensitively teased out and openly debated, can provide valuable insights as to what strategies to pursue to strengthen the position of the company in its markets.

Not fully addressing competitor impact is likely to be the result of poor-quality, or non-existent, discussions at senior level, for the following reasons.

Poor frameworks

Managers may not know how properly to analyse competitor behaviour and competitor impact. For whatever reasons, if few conversations have taken place on this subject, both the top team and the GMs are unlikely to have generated working models or frameworks to help managers understand what is happening in their markets. Part of the problem is that the senior executive – the top team and the GMs – has not really appreciated what sales and marketing mean in business. The other part of the problem is that a culture conducive to giving and receiving feedback has not been allowed to evolve and, hence, more sophisticated conversations do not take place.

Tensions

Tense and strained relationships at the top, which are due to personal, strategic or organisation structure reasons, may focus attention unduly on internal processes and issues, so that discussing competitor behaviour may hardly be considered.

Blaming

Managers may be reluctant to enter meaningfully into debate about competitor impact, as they could be accused by colleagues of incompetence. Any manager whose responsibilities cover sales, marketing, business development, or corporate or strategic direction will naturally become the centre of attention in discussions concerning the impact of competitors. Attention would probably also focus on the effectiveness of the company's own operation. In a poor-quality top team, examination of competitor impact could be sidetracked into an investigation of why the company's own managers are supposedly not performing well. Should such *blaming* happen, most managers would be discouraged from discussing the topic further.

Working in a business school provides me with access to a considerable number of different companies. It really does not take long to recognise which are the better-run companies. One indicator that I find valuable and that could easily be overlooked is listening to what is said (or unsaid) outside the lecture room. At lunch, or relaxing in the evening after a reasonably intensive day, many executive programme participants discuss competitor impact. Especially in the in-company programmes, where executives from one company are exposed to management-development programmes tailored to suit their needs, conversation concerning developments in the market is commonplace. None of the business-school jargon, such as 'competitive advantage' or 'focused differentiation', enters into the dialogue. 'How well my region is doing against the competition' prevails as a topic. GMs have developed their own sources of market intelligence, ranging from exhibitions, talking to clients, membership of local societies, and attending functions. It is impressive to listen to the detail of what others are doing in my patch, detail which emerges so naturally.

Particularly telling is what's said at the end-of-course dinner. An almost universal practice at business schools is to organise an end-of-course dinner, often the evening before the last day of the short-course programme. For the tailored, in-company programme, the guest of honour is often a senior manager from within the company, preferably the MD or the CEO. Almost inevitably, the speech given by the senior manager is followed by a question-and-answer session. The underlying health of the company is exposed in these sessions. A less than dynamic organisation is characterised by polite questioning of that senior manager, often on points of detail, by the programme participants. A more dynamic organisation is typified by cut-and-thrust discussions in which the views and knowledge of the top manager are challenged by the programme participants according to their experiences of dealing with clients and competitors. In effect, the conversation focuses on competitor impact.

A particularly dynamic top manager who encourages such challenge is Pat Hogan, Group vice-president, Northern Telecom, Europe, a subsidiary of the Canadian multinational, Northern Telecom. Pat's end-of-course dinner sessions were a highly stimulating experience in the Cranfield/Northern Telecom programmes. He asked the managers attending the course that, in their comments, they be specific in terms of whom they were talking about (client or competitor), what they had learnt, and where they had gathered their market-intelligence data. From there on, it was a no-holds-barred discussion. If you knew what you were talking about, you could say anything or challenge any senior manager on the policy of the company. Pat's encouragement of discussion concerning competitor impact, his openness of style, and his enthusiasm captivated his audience. With Pat, the end-of-course dinner became as much a training session as the more formal case study or lecture. The impact of the end-of-course dinners with Pat was twofold; firstly, the participants learned about competitors, client needs, and market trends. Secondly, the degree of motivational stimulus and identity with business, for the programme participants, increased considerably. Ten speeches on 'How well we are all doing and the promise of the future' could not have the impact of one cut-and-thrust after dinner discussion with Pat.

Pat's performance at the end-of-course dinner typified both his management style at work and his performance – since his appointment in 1987, he has achieved 30 per cent compound growth per annum for Northern Telecom Europe.

Northern Telecom is an example of a business organisation which has encouraged a culture of open discussion, and its executives develop appropriate *frameworks* for appreciating and responding to the competition. As the company has shown in terms of business performance, allow such a positive culture to develop, and the results will show. Poor top-team dynamics and ignorance concerning how to think about competitors have emerged as the main reasons why competitor impact is improperly discussed.

Not motivating people

Even if sales and marketing practices are 'right' and the organisation is 'well' structured, effective business performance is not guaranteed. Staff need to be encouraged and made constantly aware of developments in the markets and internally in the organisation, and with such insights, they must be encouraged to strive for constant improvement in performance. Hence, strategies to improve the motivation of employees to achieve increased business performance are important considerations.

Paying attention, in a professional manner, to the morale of employees is the vital link between recognising what to do and actually doing it. Yet, certain organisations simply do not recognise the relevance of identifying and implementing strategies for improving the motivation of employees. Top management may not have appreciated the relationship between motivation and business performance. To devote attention and resources to employee morale programmes may be viewed as wasteful or irrelevant.

Alternatively, the culture and history of the organisation may be ones of *cost-plus*; whatever the costs of projects and the overhead of the organisation, such costs are covered by another party. Under such circumstances, senior management are insulated from market fluctuations and hence have never been exposed to the idea of generating added value from their staff and management. Managing people, for cost-plus businesses, is synonymous with task completion and making sure the administration is 'right'. Changing the culture of a cost-plus organisation can be painful, not only because of the need to change management behaviour and attitudes, but also because the organisation is facing up to the probability of being overstaffed. Not addressing issues of motivation, suggests, by implication, that the performance of people has not been fully considered. The likely result is that mediocre performance by an overstaffed organisation becomes the norm. As has happened in so many cost-plus organisations that were previously in the public sector, privatisation suddenly exposes the ills of the past.

Lack of stakeholder awareness

If the members of the top team are not communicating clearly, or have not generated an environment in which to share and explore ideas and support each other is commonplace, their orientation is likely to be short term. Being too internally focused is also likely to lead to a neglect of key customers, suppliers, shareholders, or, in a subsidiary, key corporate headquarters executives – namely stakeholders.

Case Study 6.1

THE MD WHO BEHAVED AS A PRODUCTION MANAGER

A US consumer manufacturing organisation, Delta 2, was making a major bid to capture a substantial market share in, at least, nine European countries. Considerable resources were invested in the European operation, especially the establishment of two key plants in the Republic of Ireland. Ireland soon became the supplier of core products for the European business. The expatriate vice-president who developed the Irish manufacturing entity returned to corporate headquarters. The production manager, an Irishman, was promoted to the new role of MD, Delta 2, Ireland. The new MD's focus was product quality, coupled with a just-in-time philosophy. Bulk products needed to be tailored to customer demands, and delivered on time. The MD's track record on product quality and delivery was sound.

Although effective in managing the production process, the MD neglected to represent the Irish entity at key management forums at European headquarters in the UK and at corporate headquarters in the US. The corporation, headed by entrepreneurially oriented executives, had still not fully decided upon the shape of the European business, although the mission for greater penetration of the European market was clear and agreed. Ambitious 'young Turk' senior managers entered into the debate with enthusiasm, each hoping to carve out a fast-lane career track with new openings in Europe.

Because the MD neglected attendance at key meetings, the shape of the European business was being rapidly formed without an input from Ireland. Much to their surprise, the Irish managers learned that an alternative manufacturing site was to be built in northern Spain. Considerable overlap existed, in the product range to be manufactured in Spain, with that being manufactured in Ireland.

'Once the operation is in full swing, unit costs will be lower in Spain than in Ireland,' commented the European vice-president, marketing.

'Eamon really let this one go,' said the vice-president for corporate strategy. He continued, 'He may have been good at production, but as MD for Ireland and knowing this company, he should really have made the effort to be at the right meetings at the right time. He might be a nice guy, but in the long run, it does seem as if he let Ireland down. In this company, being good at production, important as it is, does not necessarily make you good for the top job.'

For the Irish MD (Case Study 6.1), the important stakeholders were other senior managers in the corporation. In reality, Delta 2 is an entre-preneurially oriented company. The corporation is sensitive to the opinions of its high-performing managers. Its managers have their say and do influence outcomes. The corporation holds its managers accountable for their actions, and, by implication, inactions. Whatever the economic logic of continuing with the Irish manufacturing entity, currently, Spanish manufacturing is in operation and increasing in productivity. The Irish question is being observed by a number of senior managers in the corporation. Their opinion is, 'It was Eamon's fault. He was dumb enough to let it happen!'

Important stakeholders can influence positively or negatively what happens in an organisation. They need to be identified and given sufficient attention. Especially in mid-to-large-sized multinational corporations, the key stakeholders are, more often than not, inside the corporate structure.

Impact of lack of trust at the top

Differences of values, differences of vision, and a continuing inability to offer and/or receive feedback at the top of the organisation can lead to serious problems of lack of trust among the members of the top team. The more able and motivated members of the top team may become so frustrated that one or more resign their positions. Not only do such undesired resignations demoralise those in the top team and the management levels below, but they also project a damaging image to the market, to shareholders, and to the press. If suppliers, distributors and key customers perceive the organisation as floundering because of the resignations of one or more key top managers, trust in the organisation can be damaged. Soon poor morale will spread throughout the organisation. The lack of trust in top management will become prevalent. Accompanying lack of trust, will be the lack of co-operation and support of interdepartmental and cross-functional programmes and projects. Poor response to any new initiative that involves more than one unit or department is likely to become the norm.

Poor time perspective

As a result of the above opportunity-cost problems, top managers are likely to find themselves out of touch with what is happening in the organisation, out of touch with the strength and depth of negative feeling and attitudes in the organisation, and even out of touch with what clients and key customers really feel. For managers to be 'data deprived' not only considerably aggravates an already damaging internal situation, but also makes it difficult for them to predict just how long it will take to put into operation and complete projects or programmes. In effect, top managers do not have the information and ability to visualise the time it takes to achieve particular goals.

Having a poor time perspective in terms of the business may lead to:

- inaccurately estimating the time required to nurture or develop new areas of business;
- offering commitments to clients, suppliers and distributors that are not met, and thereby alienating key business relationships;
- being unable to deliver goods and services at the times agreed.

Not being able to deliver goods or services on time and of the right quality is symptomatic of deeper problems than just scheduling. The problems emanate from fundamental issues that have remained unaddressed for some time, with the effect that opportunity-cost irritants, have turned into operational problems.

Personal costs

Openness in discussing business problems, as well as future challenges, does not necessarily involve harmonious relationships. Tension, resulting from the grit necessary to challenge ideas and proposals, may easily arise; a tension which for some may be uncomfortable but certainly not debilitating.

I think a lot of it is leadership; it is knowing when to act the heavy or the soft with somebody in private or in public; it just depends on how you do it.

Gordon Owen,
Chairman, Mercury Communications,
Group Managing Director, Cable and Wireless

Tensions within the top team need not be a problem if they arise from challenge, openness and drive to debate business options. At a personal level, relationships could be considerably negative, as long as, at a pro-fessional/business level, managers' respect for each other and identity with the business lead to the robustness necessary for positive discourse.

Tension that arises from poor-quality business relationships is consid-erably damaging both businesswise and personally. At least, when the business relationships are fundamentally sound, if a senior manager feels uncomfortable within the top team, he can leave. When the business relationships are basically unsound; when the discussion that should be taking place is not taking place, it may be difficult to leave. Under such circumstances, costs at a personal level are likely to occur.

Personal costs mean the emotional trauma experienced by a manager who has to shoulder the negative emotions of others; to work in circum-stances in which he does not have the necessary accountabilities and responsibilities to do his job; or to exist in an environment when patch-ing up problems, being undermined, and being over-sensitive to what is said or what to say, are the norm. The individual senior manager may be accused of not being a team player or of being selfishly motivated. On closer examination, this may be found not to be the case, as anyone in a similar situation would have acted comparably.

Hence, not only is the manager not appreciated for his contribution, but he may also suffer a form of personal abuse. Being exposed, for any length of time, to such an environment may, for some, lead to loss of confidence, while others learn to survive unharmed. Loss of confidence to act is likely to lead to loss of motivation and drive, leaving the manager feeling emotionally vulnerable most of the time. Most senior managers who have experienced such damaging emotions can hide their true mental state, at work, for considerable periods of time. They are unlikely to hide what they really feel at home. It does not take long for the stresses and strains of work to emerge at home, leading to damaged familial relation-ships.

In extreme circumstances, the manager may experience some form of personal breakdown. The majority, however, do not break down; but in a negative culture, they have not learnt personal maturity. What they have learnt is to suppress anxieties, but their emotions are bubbling just under the surface. One can feel low for a long time – in effect, a lifetime – constantly performing under par – always giving one's second best. Not sorting out the business, damages the business. It also damages the people!

MINIMISING THE DAMAGE

The fundamental theme of this book has been *the top team*. To repeat the message, the interviews, case studies and survey results over-whelmingly show that the top team is the fundamental source of influence for the effective running of the business. Other factors add to, or limit, the impact of the top team. The survey results also strongly emphasise that the seven areas of opportunity cost are the result of poor top-team behaviour and performance. Of all the results, the strongest correlations emerge when examining the impact of a poor top team on the business, as shown below.

Survey results

		Not market responsive
		Poorly configured structure
		Low follow-through
NEGATIVE TOP TEAM →	DISARRAY →	Poor internal controls
		Low strategic insight
		Poor morale

A negative top team (it is insensitive, does not communicate, does not address known sensitivities, is short-term oriented; its members are immature – the list could continue) generates a culture of disarray. The organisation is marked by poor internal systems and controls, and a management that lacks discipline and does not really understand the business outside its own functional area; its managers are moved on too quickly; and, generally, its internal administration is seen as disruptive and disabling, a perception which, in turn, directly affects key perform-ance factors. Under such circumstances, staff and management become less and less market responsive.

The situation is classic. Since the basics have not been sorted out, the fire-fighting mentality emerges – for good reason – there are many fires to fight. Short termism becomes the dominant strategic focus, not only for the top team, but for the levels of management immediately below. Senior managers do not develop within themselves the insights neces-sary for meaningful and pragmatic debate about medium-to-long-term options. For those who have not nurtured the insights necessary for strategic thinking, such debate is synonymous with 'pie in the sky' conversations.

Minimising damage to the business requires coming to terms with the source of the damage. It is then necessary for someone to start a discussion – why are we doing things wrong? The insights and information necessary to hold a discussion of what's wrong is available – it can be found in the perceptions, experiences and feelings within the members of the top team and among the GMs.

BEST PRACTICE INVENTORY

Dos

- [ ] Create a positive culture. Supporting fundamental values of being professional and business-like, externally and internally, is basic to developing a culture focused on success.

- [ ] Generate an environment where there is confidence to act. For such an environment to develop, middle- and lower-level management need to trust top management. In order to respond appropriately, top managers need to show that they are in touch with the issues and concerns of managers down the line. A culture of upward communication needs to emerge through the managerial hierarchy. Because top managers have been able to develop the behaviours of managing improved communications, does not mean that middle- and lower-level managers could respond positively. Hence, initiatives concerning upward communication need to be supported by strategies for training and developing those levels of management concerned.

- [ ] Generate an environment where quality of service counts. Quality of service is not just improving performance on particular tasks; it is an overall philosophy – a way of life. Improvements in individual and organisational performance need to be addressed and rewarded. What quality of service means and the standards to be attained need to be documented. Furthermore, quality of service needs to be driven from the top, not only in terms of leadership, but also in terms of participation. Top management must be seen to be practising quality of service themselves.

- [ ] Generate an environment where 'people count'. Communicating, listening and managing meetings well are integral elements of a positive and professional people-oriented culture. The slogan 'people count' does not mean that a social organisation is being created at work. A culture in which 'people count' is one where professional discipline, respect and maturity are enhanced in order that a realistic belief in long-term success is shared by staff and management. Often is heard

185

the saying, 'our most important asset is our people'. Making best use of that asset is generating a culture in which 'people count'.

☐ Be aware of what damage can be done. Poor performance within the top team can induce any one or more of seven areas of opportunity cost.

Don'ts

☐ Do not allow a negative situation to continue. Problems that induce opportunity costs are likely to be the result of poor performance in the top team. Ways need to be found to address such concerns. True, certain sensitivities may take time to address, and that has to be allowed for. At the end of the day, however, the members of the top team need to find a way of talking to each other.

It sounds simple – have a talk – you have all the data you need. In reality, it is very difficult to discuss something that has remained undiscussed for a considerable time. If people have been unable to come to terms with their problems, how can they change and improve overnight?

Addressing such crucial and sensitive issues needs to be accompanied by a strategy for *executive development*.

7

Executive Development

Training is like an injection of blood into the system. It is essential but it is easy not to do. It really is ground bait. The fertiliser of the future. If you go round our people you can see . . . their commitment to the business that comes out of a couple of weeks at Heythrop [Park], having their eyes opened to their capabilities . . . It does me a hell of a lot of good to go there.

Tom Frost,
CEO,
National Westminster Bank

Tom Frost is referring to Heythrop Park, the main NatWest training centre, set in the Oxfordshire countryside. Between £50 and £60m per annum is spent by NatWest on training, which does not include on-the-job learning, or the indirect costs of staff and management being away from work. Such investment is considered well spent!

The development of any organisation's management is crucial to its long-term success and prosperity. As has been constantly emphasised throughout this book, the actions, behaviours, attitudes and quality of relationships of top and middle management have a substantial impact on the organisation. Guiding managers in thinking about their role and how to behave within the role provides a vital contribution to the development of the business. What can be done to develop managers who hold high office or those who exhibit the potential for top posts? In addition to the Top Executive Survey and the results of a number of other Cranfield surveys, the original ones spearheaded by Charles Margerison and myself identified ways for developing actual, potential and latent executive capacity.*

---

* Certain ideas in this chapter are taken from Margerison, CJ and Kakabadse, AP (1984) *How American Chief Executives Succeed*. AMA Survey Report.

THE CHARACTERISTICS OF UK AND US CEOs

Demographic data

Two surveys indicate that, on average, high-calibre executives attain a senior management position by the age of 32. The average age at appointment to CEO is slightly younger in the US (39.4 years) than in the UK (41.0 years). There seems to be a critical eight–nine year period of rapid development in senior managers before they are considered suitable for a top position. On average, managers of top-executive calibre have been employed in from three to four separate organisations and have held nine separate jobs.

Management development needs

Six key factors indicating the emphasis that needs to be placed in management development were identified, as shown in the following table.

Table 7.1 *Key issues for management development*

US chief executives	UK chief executives
1. Need to achieve results.	1. Ability to work with a wide variety of people.
2. Ability to work with a wide variety of people.	2. Substantial responsibility for important tasks.
3. Challenge.	3. Need to achieve results.
4. Willingness to take risks.	4. Leadership experience early in career.
5. Early overall responsibility for important tasks.	5. Width of experience in many functions before age 35.
6. Width of experience in many functions before age 35.	6. Ability to do deals and negotiate.

Three separate categories can be identified from the results outlined in the table above: relationship management, personal drive, and career planning.

Relationship management

Factors such as the ability to work with a wide variety of people, the ability to do deals and negotiate, and leadership experience early in one's career, support the Top Executive Survey findings which indicate that senior managers consider that the ability to manage people effectively is important in job performance. The UK respondents place slightly greater emphasis on managing people skills than do the US respondents. In these two studies, the respondents were asked what were the most important aspects of their job they had to learn to perform their role as an executive. The interpersonal factors of communication, delegation and patience emerged as the main items. Therefore, the ability to work with a wide variety of people is something which CEOs feel they have to work hard at, and it is a crucial element of their own personal development.

Personal drive

Factors such as the need to achieve results, challenge and a willingness to take risks, emphasise the importance senior managers attach to energy, drive and commitment. The US top manager attaches greater importance to personal drive, in contrast to the UK, who attaches greater value to relationship management.

Career planning

It is felt by most managers that an important influence on their own executive development is having had responsibility for important aspects of the organisation's work early in their career. In most cases this would mean a profit-and-loss responsibility for a unit. Furthermore, a wide experience of the various functions in the organisation before the age of 35 is important if that person is destined for senior management. The organisational implication is that people should be encouraged to apply their skills in other functions to attain the breadth of experience necessary for leadership responsibility. Numerous managers indicated to us how much they had learned by crossing organisational boundaries and recognising how business functions need to be integrated at a senior level. Clearly, it is not possible for everyone to have this opportunity, but it is important for staff who are to undertake policy-level work to have experience in at least two or three functions other than their own specialist professional areas. In order to provide a breadth of experience as an essential ingredient in executive development, forward thinking is required on both the manager's part and the organisation's.

STRATEGIES FOR EXECUTIVE DEVELOPMENT

To summarise, top managers:

- need to understand their business intimately by having managed more than one function;

- need to form a vision as to the shape and direction of the function, or organisation, for which they are accountable;

- need to communicate clearly the mission of the organisation and objectives to be achieved;

- need to structure clearly the jobs of their managers and staff;

- need to display tact and sensitivity in managing people and teams;

- need to consider how to communicate and identify appropriate channels for communication;

- need to make themselves available to receive feedback;

- need to behave in ways that support the policies and objectives they wish others to adopt;

- must work on numerous activities simultaneously;

- must work under pressure in situations of diversity, complexity and change;

- must implement ideas, policies and activities through individuals and groups;

- should support and encourage the training of staff and lower levels of management by providing job- and career-related development opportunities;

- should be concerned about their own development.

I present six strategies for the training and development of managers which utilise these guidelines.

1. Feedback and executive development
2. Working with consultants
3. The manager as a high achiever
4. Development through training
5. Presentation skills
6. Personal development time

Feedback and executive development

A key executive development strategy is *feedback*, whether offered to individuals or to teams. As stressed in Chapters 5 and 6, feedback is the crucial mechanism for adjusting and improving performance on the job.

No matter how aware the manager, there are limits to recognising just how far one needs to go to improve. Someone else needs to offer his views as to the effectiveness of a manager's or group's performance, accompanied by recommendations for improvement. If one is involved in doing a job, ie completing a task of a specialist or managerial nature, feedback is desirable, if for no other reason than to tell the manager when he is going wrong. At least with operational work, the manager could deduce when he may be making mistakes, and adjust his performance. Of course, being offered feedback helps.

In strategic work, the need for feedback is that much greater. Making the right strategic choice is as much a statement of belief, as it is logical deduction from quantifiable data. As much depends on selling ideas internally, on the ability to project an appropriate image through effective communication, as on emerging with theoretically the 'right' solution. The behaviour of the members of the senior executive directly influences the beliefs others have in the mission and the strategies of the organisation. The more feedback senior managers can invite and digest, the more conscious they will be of the impact they make in the management of the mission strategy and structure of the organisation (Figure 7.1 on page 192). Hence, managing the process of giving and receiving feedback at senior level is crucial for the continued growth and progress of the business.

While Chapter 5 has concentrated on examining the feedback process at the individual level, and Chapter 6 has focused on what is required to generate upward communication in the organisation, this chapter examines how feedback can be utilised as a tool for executive development. Developing managers to participate effectively in the feedback process involves examining their capacity for self-understanding, examining their ability to handle appraisals, and assisting executive teams to respond well to team feedback.

Self-understanding

As top managers attribute much of their success to personal style and managing interfaces, it is important for them to realise their strengths and weaknesses, their skills and styles which need further development and training, and their capacity to manage complex relationships. Towards this end, there are various tests, questionnaires and exercises which are widely used, and which act as a positive stimulus to most senior managers. The value of these tests is that they tend to highlight key issues concerning abilities, attitudes, managerial style and more fundamental aspects of personality, insights which the manager has probably suspected, but which have not been sufficiently emphasised or confirmed.

191

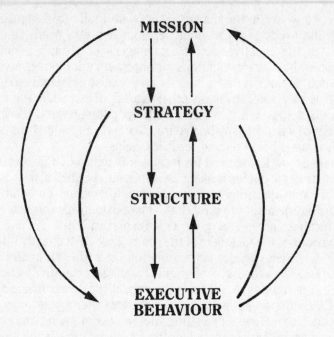

Figure 7.1 *Executive competencies*

A further benefit of such tests is that differences between senior managers can be identified. Each manager is likely to develop his own particular style and approach to managing people and situations. Problems can occur in organisations when one manager does not understand or appreciate the managerial style and strengths of a colleague or the constraints under which the other manager operates. Such problems may lead to a lack of cooperation and mistrust. Utilising tests can be of immense value in improving relationships, by helping each senior manager understand that different people adopt different approaches to solving problems. Once managers gain certain insights concerning the styles and skills of others, poor working relationships can be repaired.

Personal development and the effective use of tests can be formalised in development centres which adopt a career development philosophy. The traditional assessment centres attempt to *identify* high-flyers by using tests, questionnaires and exercises. Such assessment centres are of only limited value. Identifying potential top managers is one thing. Developing the capacity for high office is far more useful. The most powerful form of assessment is one directly related to job performance.

Hence, if the assessment centre experience is used as an opportunity for people to consider their abilities, strengths and weaknesses, and identify appropriate action plans for themselves, then a great deal has been achieved. It is strongly advocated that the emphasis should be on development rather than on assessment.

A key finding in the Cranfield surveys is that top managers are self-developed, but, most certainly they are *not born*. The evidence indicates that if the assessment centre process is utilised for discussion and personal development, ie as a development centre, rather than simply to label individuals as high flyers, high-performing executives will emerge.

Appraisal process

The development of any manager depends on his consistency and periodically being offered feedback on performance, with an opportunity to discuss with the boss ways of improving on the job. Effective appraisal does not depend so much on the scope and subtlety of the appraisal form, as on the attitudes and sensitivity of top management. If top managers value the appraisal process, they should both practise it themselves and push the practice of conducting proper appraisals down the line. Some of the questions top managers need to ask are the following:

- To what extent are appraisals really valued in the organisation?

- To what extent do senior managers require middle managers to conduct effective appraisals throughout the organisation?

- Is the appraisal process squeezed in between other pressing commitments?

- Do senior managers themselves undergo appraisal?

- Are middle- and junior-level managers aware that top managers themselves undergo appraisal?

- Are managers given feedback, or are they appraised, on their ability to conduct appraisals?

- Do the results of appraisal form a normal distribution? ie not all managers are marked 'excellent' or 'very good'. Are those who have performed poorly identified as such, and given that feedback?

If the answer to most of these questions is no, then it is likely that the appraisal process is poorly conducted in the organisation, and that a key development opportunity for line management is consistently being underutilised. Under such circumstances, line managers are likely to be less trusting of top managers, to be ignorant of their own shortcomings, to resent the fact that top managers may make demands for improvement, and generally to identify less with the strategies and mission of the organisation.

The most effective appraisal is one conducted on a daily or weekly basis, especially on an informal basis, so that appraisal becomes a way of life as opposed to an annual, formal event.

Team feedback

As considerable work is conducted on a team basis, and as more policies, strategies and decisions are made and implemented within team settings, teams, like individuals, require development. A particularly potent development experience is *team feedback*. For top teams especially, the feedback process needs to encompass feedback to individuals and feedback on how the quality of interactions among team members affects the management and business growth of the organisation.

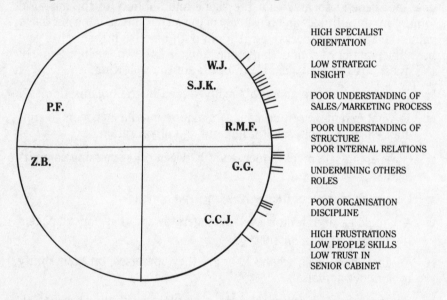

Figure 7.2 *Team grid: the Kappa Z team*

In order to capture both people and business data in one feedback process, the research team and I developed the *Top Team Grid*. The team grid is a feedback tool which attempts to capture the skills and weaknesses of individual top managers, their personal impact on their function and overall organisation, and how their quality of relationship within the team enhances or constrains the growth and progress of the organisation. In order to make a powerful impact in terms of feedback, each individual on the team grid is identified by name.

Case Study 7.1

THE KAPPA Z TEAM

The MD of Kappa Z, (pseudonym of an information technology company), requested help, stating that he faced major problems in his senior team. He saw his immediate subordinates as specialist engineers, who were immature as people, basically unaware of how to manage key business and commercial processes, and unable to work together as a business team. He believed himself to be seen by the team as unpopular, out of step with his colleagues, unreasonable, and holding back progress.

The results of further interviews certainly supported the MD's view that his people had of him – they saw him as a difficult and ineffective leader. The MD, other team members, and financial performance indicators all strongly supported the view that the business was going downhill. The team, however, did agree to undergo a two-day development programme, focusing on providing feedback on the quality of the team members' relationships and their capacity to manage the business. They all agreed to complete the team grid.

The grid results were interesting (Figure 7.2). Three of the functional directors of Kappa Z – WJ, SJK, RMF – were described as too specialist, as lacking the necessary insights to be effective at strategic thinking, as having a poor understanding of sales and marketing, as not appreciating how to operate the organisational structure, and as having poor relations with their colleagues on the team and also with their immediate subordinates. The two remaining functional directors – CCJ and GG – were described as undermining the roles of others, as poorly disciplined in terms of meeting deadlines and attending meetings, as not trusting their colleagues in the senior team, as poorly skilled at managing people, and as frustrated with their job. The deputy MD – PF – emerged from the analysis as a pleasant man, supportive of others, well disciplined, good at managing people, trusting his colleagues, and, despite all the problems, displaying a positive attitude to the job. The MD – ZB – emerged as considerably different from the others. He was described as a generalist, as sensitive to the processes of strategic discussion and having the insight to recognise long-term strategic developments, as having a good understanding of the sales and marketing process, as understanding how to operate the structure, as not undermining the position and roles of colleagues, as well disciplined, as trusting of colleagues, and as well skilled at handling people. In fact, ZB and PF exhibited the opposite characteristics to the rest of the team. As can be seen, ZB and PF stood out from all the rest. Furthermore, the grid showed the growing distance of ZB and PF from each other and from the rest of the team. Because of the tensions and back-room politics in the team, PF, much as a result of his lack of strategic insight, was slowly becoming more sympathetic to the positions of the functional directors and was losing rapport with his boss. ZB was isolated from the group. Everyone else thought he was the problem! In reality, *they* were the problem!

195

> The team members were called together to attend the two-day workshop held in a hotel. On the morning of the first day, the key concepts behind the grid were explained to the group. Each member received a copy of the grid, which identified the team members by name and listed their strengths and weaknesses. It was accompanied by a summary report giving the opportunity costs and likely damage to the business should the situation remain the same.
>
> The group members stared at the grid, as it shone on the screen from the overhead projector.
>
> 'Bloody hell, that's us,' muttered SFK.
>
> 'Hell, that's me,' said WJ, referring to his being described as having a poor understanding of the sales and marketing process. WJ was the sales director.
>
> 'Well, gentlemen, let me have your initial thoughts and views,' requested the consultant.

It is unrealistic to expect people in trouble to have the ability and motivation to be capable of utilising feedback data. Giving feedback to induce positive outcomes needs to be guided through the four stages described in the following paragraphs.

Shock

The majority of the members of the team of Kappa Z in Case Study 7.1 were shocked on receiving the feedback. That is a natural response which needs to be managed to help the members make use of the data that has been offered to them. The self-identity of the members and the identity of the team itself has been challenged. Managers, both as people and as responsible executives were being told that they were quite different from how they perceived themselves. Even ZB was shocked. His 'gut feeling' was that it was his team, not he, that was at fault. However, to see that clearly expressed on paper – to have your gut feeling spelt out – and then to recognise just how divorced one had become from one's colleagues and how futile is communication through words, would be a blow to anyone. Although the initial shock on receiving feedback, especially in front of one's colleagues, is disorienting, it is also an opportunity to begin to remove outdated assumptions, behaviours and attitudes which harm the relationships among the members of the senior team.

Rejection and denial

Rejection of the data and denial of the problem, as responses from managers whose identity has been challenged, are commonplace reactions. A senior manager feeling threatened could say any of the following:

■ The data are inaccurate.

■ You missed something in your analysis.

■ You didn't get the real picture because here's what's good about our place (PF's response).

■ Just how valid is the methodology? (CCJ's response).

■ You really just got it wrong – we're not like that (as two of the Kappa Z directors stated).

Rejection and denial are part of the feedback process. For an external facilitator, this part of the feedback process is likely to be an uncomfortable experience, for the credibility of the data and of the facilitator are being seriously questioned. The facilitator should try to talk the group through this stage rather than attempt to defend the feedback data or himself. To overcome denial, the facilitator may adopt one or more of the following strategies:

■ Encourage discussion of the data to allow the group members to 'talk out' their negative feelings in order to reach a point where they are more prepared to consider the implications of the data.

■ Depending on the size of the team, treat it as one group or divide it into two or more subgroups. Then focus the discussion by asking the subgroups to prepare a SWOT (strengths, weaknesses, opportunities, threats) analysis of the business in which the team grid feedback data or, for that matter, any feedback data, such as consultancy reports, are simply one more input into the debate. Have each of the subgroups prepare a presentation of their discussion and present it to the other subgroups. Once all presentations are complete, have the top team, as a group, distil the key messages from each subgroup's findings in order jointly to discuss what remedial actions, over the short, medium and long term, the team should take to overcome the problems facing the organisation. The Kappa Z team adopted this line in order to explore further the feedback data.

■ Use psychological tests, exercises and any other management-development techniques. They can be effective mechanisms both to provide managers with the basic tools and concepts to understand organisational processes, and to take the sting out of sensitive discussions. Utilising management-development techniques to facilitate discussion within the team is a safe route to considering the implications of feedback to the team or to individuals. The approach at

Cranfield is to combine team grid feedback with feedback and learning from 'safer' exercises, tests or case studies.

■ Patiently build up a robustness of relationship among the members of the top team to enable them to handle feedback data. During the process of gathering data, it will be necessary to assess the ability of each member of the top team to cope with and benefit from feedback. Perseverance, timing and personal patience are required to work on the relationships in order to improve each manager's capacity to benefit from the feedback process. It could take days, weeks or even months to build up participants to the point where they could enter into a feedback dialogue and learn, rather than collapse, from the experience. What to do in the meantime, how to maintain credibility with the client, and how still to produce and show useful output during this period, certainly tests the skills of the consultant.

■ Know when to *back off* to prevent the whole intervention from collapsing. Feedback, although crucial to the development of the top team and, by implication, the overall business, may not be an experience the client wishes to undergo, despite the attention offered by the consultant. Alternative development activities or terminating the intervention altogether, may be required. A manager who does not wish to hear is likely to reject feedback data, and to deny he has problems. It is important to prevent too much hostility from being generated, as all chance of team development, through feedback, for the future, may be destroyed.

Need to talk

Once feedback has been given and the uncomfortable stage of rejection and denial has been worked through, managers may need to talk through, time and again, the content of the feedback data, the relevance of the data, the personal implication for them of that data, and what is required to adjust and improve. Although not all would wish to talk the same issues through repeatedly, some managers would. Hence, willingness to meet managers on a regular basis, or sporadically on request, needs to be exhibited by the consultant. Making oneself available and/ or contactable after the feedback event, by offering follow-up counselling, assists the feedback learning process. To make sense of the data sufficient to change behaviour, or to introduce or change policies, means that the manager has to rethink and relearn. Uncertainty, lack of confidence, and a need to think through in detail new and alternative approaches, testing out new ideas, are natural experiences after feedback. Certainly, in the case of Kappa Z, PF, WJ and GG held long and numerous meetings with the consultant. For PF, the results of the discussion helped him come to terms with his role of deputy MD and his lack of strategic thinking. WJ recognised how much he wanted to be a specialist and not a generalist, and, over a period of time, he negotiated a role within Kappa Z more suited to his talents. GG slowly came to terms with the fact that he had, in reality, been unhappy at Kappa Z. To his relief, he admitted that to himself and left the organisation.

The availability of a counsellor, so that managers can bounce ideas off a 'safe' and trusted person, is valuable for their learning and internalising what actions are required to introduce change.

Owning the strategies for action

The ultimate purpose of feedback is for the managers to 'own' the final strategies for action. Whether these strategies for action were originally conceived and initiated by top managers, or offered to them by external agents, the purpose behind the feedback process is for top managers to be committed to the strategies for action on change. Reaching the point of ownership and commitment to change and identifying the strategies for change depend as much on the logic and viability of the data, as on the manner in which the data feedback process is managed. Depending on the circumstances and the individual managers involved, it may be more important to pay attention to the logic and quantifiable aspects of the data, or to the processes of data feedback, people's responses, and offering support and counselling. If greater attention needs to be given to process, it is not unusual for individual members or the team concerned to pursue the most *comfortable*, as opposed to the ideal, strategies for change. Owning the actions necessary to improve depends on what the team members feel they can perform. Depending on what the team feel they can perform may mean implementing the second or third preferred solution, as a stepping stone towards effective change.

Consultants involved in this stepping-stone approach to change need to think long term and be able to manage ambiguity. For managers within the organisation, who may be attempting to introduce change through feedback and in so doing have adopted the role of consultant, the same issues and processes apply except that, as internal-change agents, they have to be that much more careful and sensitive. Consultants can, at the end of the day, walk away. The internal-change agents have to live with the consequences.

Working with consultants

Utilising tests and questionnaires, developing individuals and teams, and gathering and offering for further debate information about the organisation, its people, products and impact on the market, require that the third parties who may be utilised have business experience and behavioural science expertise. The nature of consultancy is changing, becoming more professional, and making greater demands on consultants.

Expert consultants require expert knowledge and experience to be able to apply their knowledge base in different client circumstances.

Consultants who are more involved in strategic development, policy implementation, and business development will need insight as to 'what's right' for the business as well as an understanding of how to handle the people involved. From the client's point of view, the consultant should have some behavioural science understanding; he should, if necessary, be qualified to administer tests and provide counselling, feedback and analysis on a personal or group basis, or be a member of a team offering such services. Although this more personalised approach to consultancy has been available for a considerable time, many senior managers have not made use of it. Many managers still see consultants as persons hired to examine situations and then submit reports. Involvement at the implementation stage is a practice still not sufficiently commonly widespread. Such consultants, however, are necessary, in order to facilitate the ownership of and commitment to the policies and strategies to be pursued.

The manager as a high achiever

The need to achieve results is given high priority by top managers. This is the factor which they consider to have the strongest influence in their own management development. It is therefore important in developing successful managers that the various ways in which such achievement is identified can be utilised for development purposes. Few organisations actually try to measure a manager's need to achieve results. Tests exist which explore an executive's need to achieve results. Such tests are useful when one does not know the track record of a manager. They are therefore helpful in selecting personnel when they are joining an organisation straight from university or college, or moving to an organisation in mid-career.

One would not normally consider applying such tests to managers who have been with an organisation for a period of time. Their achievement should be measured through actual performance rather than through tests. Track record, after all, is one of the best indicators of future performance. However, where this track record is not easily evaluated, as in the case of newcomers joining an organisation, the application of need-for-achievement tests, as one factor in determining whether managers are likely to have the necessary attitude and determination to succeed is recommended. Such tests in themselves do not give an answer. They will only give an indication of a candidate's basic orientation, which together with interview data can make an important contribution to making decisions which can cost the organisation large sums of money over a number of years.

The second aspect of the need to achieve is that such a need can be encouraged and stimulated through training. While this is no doubt true, it is no substitute for a person's natural desire to achieve results and set high standards and targets. One of the key aspects of being an effective manager is to encourage others to achieve results and improve upon previous performance. Therefore, it could be useful to have senior managers involved in such achievement training, if only so that they know how to develop and stimulate others to improve their own achievement levels.

Practical experience and the high-performing manager

The job of managing, like so many other things in life, is learned primarily by doing. It is therefore vital that those managers who are moving towards senior positions have the opportunity to acquire the necessary experience at the right time. There are a number of key points which must be built into the manpower-planning framework of an organisation rather than be left to chance.

Challenge

The first of these is to create jobs which enable managers to have a challenging job and overall responsibility for running part of the business. In this sense, there is an advantage in ensuring that organisations are not too centralised. It is of advantage for the organisation to divide up its work into profit-and-loss units so that managers can obtain the experience of running an operation which, while interdependent with the rest of the organisation, stands on its own as a measurable business centre.

Some businesses lend themselves to this form of organisation; for example, the retail industry where managers can often, at a young age, take on the management of shops with a considerable volume of turnover. It is perhaps more difficult to break the organisation up into such similar economic units in the process and other technologically sophisticated industries. However, wherever possible, economic units should be established so that young managers can have the experience of leading a team; so that they know 'the buck stops' with them for the overall performance of their subordinates. The key issue is that jobs for managers in their 20s and 30s should involve tasks where they can be stretched. The manager should have clear goals to work towards. Learning from doing should be the philosophy. On this basis, it is important that managers receive regular feedback on their performance in order to gain the guidance and constructive criticism necessary for improvement.

Early leadership experience

The second area of practical experience for prospective leaders must be in the area of personal leadership. This means managing a team. Unless a manager can learn how to allocate work, resolve differences of opinion, chair meetings, encourage people, address conflicts, and be held accountable for the decisions he has made, all practical leadership tasks, then he is less likely to move to high office with confidence, or to be effective in his present position. It has often been said that management is about getting things done through persuasion. The way to learn this is to gain a leadership post early in one's career.

Most of the managers in the Margerison and Kakabadse study felt this must come before the age of 30 and preferably around 25. Two-thirds of the respondents had received their first leadership post before 30, with all but 10 per cent being in such a position before 35. However, perhaps the most interesting finding of the Margerison and Kakabadse study is that 41 per cent of respondents had, in fact, gained their first leadership post before 25.

In an age of professional specialists in which people spend a long period in the formal educational process, it is perhaps difficult to gain leadership experience early in one's career. However, manpower planning and the design of the organisational structure can facilitate the creation of leadership positions.

Wider organisational perspective

The third practical experience that prospective leaders need is a wider view of their business. This can only be gained by having experience in more than one of the business functions at a relatively early age. A common complaint is that too many people are held for too long in the area of their original technical training. For example, engineers who spend all their time in the production function are unlikely to have developed the basic awareness necessary for general management. Another example is offered by accountants, who spend virtually all of their time in the finance function without learning much about marketing, sales, personnel, or production.

If senior managers are to learn how to run an integrated business, it is vitally important that they have experience in two or three functions of the business before the age of 35. For example, a marketing manager could be placed in a support function such as human resources or another line function such as production. Likewise, a production manager could well develop rapidly by working for a period in the marketing area. These moves should be planned rather than *ad hoc*.

In addition, managers with high potential should be allocated to project groups, working parties and task forces which enable them to develop a wider view of the business operation in a practical way by working on specific tasks.

Development through training

As can be seen from the survey results, concepts of strategy and executive development are becoming ever more crucial for organisation development. Managers need to keep up to date. As progress is rapid, middle and senior managers are, from now on, likely to experience continuous education as an integral part of their working life.

With the time constraints faced by managers, continuous education needs to be considered as part of a planned process of continuing development. For management education to be considered effective, the following ingredients must be present:

- Management education needs to be integrated into the career plan of the individuals concerned.

- Management education needs to address the problems faced by managers in their organisation.

Consequently, a portfolio of training experiences needs to be available for managers, ranging from specialist seminars and workshops, to short courses, to longer training experiences such as Master of Business Administration (MBA) programmes.

Long short courses

Over the last five years, the short course of five or six weeks' duration has become less popular. Taking that much time off work is generally viewed by managers as lavish in relation to the added value gained for the individual and the business. However, the longer short course can be an important influence in developing the potential in those who exhibit general management capacity, if the elements discussed in the following paragraphs are incorporated in the programme.

Issues-based teaching in terms of how the various specialisms are presented. A strategic perspective needs to be taken in the presentation of the key subject areas of finance, marketing/sales, information technology, manufacturing/design, and human resources, with strategy as the subject matter binding the others together to form a cohesive identity for the programme.

International and research-based teaching materials and concepts are no longer a luxury for managers of mid- to large-sized corporations. Teaching inputs which comprise trends and practices across key markets and provide up-to-date information, inputs which by implication require substantial investment in research, will distinguish the high-quality management education institution from other colleges. Added value, in terms of management education for the future, will depend on research results of a cross-comparative nature.

A broader societal perspective needs to be adopted in order to stimulate an understanding of the key relationships between business and society. Esoteric sociological and political science lectures are not the issue. Fundamental and pragmatic teaching inputs will be required on those aspects of society which the business world influences and those societal developments which the business world cannot ignore. Topics such as acid rain, Third World dumping, world politics and its impact on economic trends, and business in Europe before and after 1992 are important elements in any top executive development programme. From this perspective, a model programme for the development of senior managers from the private and public sectors is the *Top Management Programme*. The Top Management Programme is a cabinet office initiative, bringing together senior civil servants and high-flyers from the private sector to appreciate and learn from a high-quality, internationally based faculty and from each other, not only the practicalities of management at the top, what works and what does not, but also how the others approach the key issues. For managers who work in mid- to large-sized corporations, taking a broader societal perspective provides the tools for considering medium- to long-term strategic developments, and, in effect, makes issues such as business ethics and corporate responsibility realistic concerns rather than ephemeral subjects.

Making contacts with other programme participants, during and after the programme, is an important element of executive development programmes. The calibre of the programme participants, and their experiences are important ingredients in the success of a programme. Such a formula was uppermost in the mind of John Mayne, the senior civil servant who founded the Top Management Programme, and in the minds of the subsequent programme directors, Hayden Phillips, Brian Gilmore and Marianne Neville-Rolfe, all of whom recognised that the ties and friendships established between private-sector executives and senior government personnel would not only be a valuable developmental experience for the participants on the programme, but would also be an informal and powerful network strengthening ties between government and industry. Learning from each other and forming mentorship relationships, can make lasting impacts on each manager.

Personal development is the foundation for an executive-development programme. A high-calibre programme should bring together quantitative learning inputs such as strategy, functional business skills, and economic and political trends, with more qualitative concerns such as the personality of the manager and how that affects his performance and decision-making capacity, the importance of management style, and how attitude can be a powerful enabler or inhibitor to individual and team performance. Personal counselling, the use of psychological and management-style tests, and even well-planned outdoor activities, are fruitful mechanisms for helping managers understand what they are like personally, how they operate, and what further on-the-job development experiences they need to undergo in order to stimulate greater improvement. If we do not bring subject-matter content together with personal feedback and counselling, learning remains too much at a cerebral level with no guarantee that such learning will be applied in the workplace. Once learning becomes an emotional experience, especially if the manager is receiving feedback on his capacity to shape an identity for the function or organisation for which he is accountable, or on how differences of personality and perspectives adopted could severely inhibit discussion within the top team, or dampen the enthusiasm of others, it is likely that an impact will be made on that manager's performance at work. Each participant internalises learning and gives serious consideration to what he will do on return to work. Hence, considerable time needs to be structured into the programme for group and individual counselling and feedback.

Placements and visits are an effective mechanism for broadening experience. Business schools tend to place less emphasis on placements and visits, often because of the inhibiting costs that can be incurred, both financially and administratively. In contrast, certain public-sector bodies value highly the learning gained from in-depth visits. Again, the Top Management Programme offers a choice of placement to participants, whereby that experience has to be written up and discussed on their return. The Senior Command Course at the National Police Training College, Bramshill, requires that officers who are being prepared for top rank be exposed to the issues, concerns and challenges of different organisations. Such experiences make a powerful impact, especially on those managers who are about to enter senior office. With the rapidly changing face of Europe, placements and visits on the Continent in both government and private sector would be invaluable exposure for UK executives, especially since *only 33 per cent* of the respondents in the Top Executive Survey described their organisation as actively preparing for 1992. The remaining companies reported a more reactive position, in terms of offering a greater number of existing goods and services, exploring possibilities of consolidating their position in their home markets, or having given little consideration to Europeanisation whatsoever.

The MBA

Master of Business Administration (MBA) programmes are growing in popularity in Europe. Programmes are offered on a full-time and now part-time basis. In the latter the student remains in employment and attends MBA classes in the evening or at weekends, for a period of two, three or more years. Like the well-organised and thoughtfully focused short course of longer duration, the MBA tends to have a profound, long-term impact. In fact, the survey results reveal differences between managers who have and those who have not attended business school MBA programmes. These results are summarised in the following table:

Business school education and the senior manager: survey results

Non-attendees	*Attendees*
■ Specialist oriented	■ General management oriented
■ Functional identity	
■ Right and wrong way of doing things	■ Sensitive to corporate identity
■ Respect subordinates who stick to rules	■ High emphasis on communication
■ Subordinates should follow established procedures	■ Responsive to feelings and attitudes of others
■ Communications on a need-to-know basis	■ Emphasis on winning others over
■ Systems and controls are a hindrance	■ Spend time checking meanings
■ Few receive performance-related feedback	■ 'Bed down' the structure
	■ Generally around and available

Those who have *not* attended business school tend to rely more on a control philosophy for management, identifying more with specialist aspects of their job, the function for which they are accountable, and the exercise of authority. They rely less on negotiation, winning commitment, and communicating with people. Attendees of business schools, on either MBA or short courses, tend to be more sensitive to nurturing key interfaces, winning people over, projecting a corporate identity, and holding a general-management perspective on the management of the organisation and its personnel.

Those who have been exposed to management development are likely to spend more time considering how to give identity and focus to their role in terms of integrating functional identities with the corporate mission. They are more likely to be sensitive to issues of structure, reorganisation, strategy, follow-through, and after-care. Whatever has been planned and designed, those who have been through training are likely to make the time for consultation and support in order to make strategies and structures 'work'.

Tailor-made experiences

An increasingly popular practice is for management-education institutions to make a conscious effort to address the needs of single client organisations. Close association between business-education institutions and business organisations occurs, whereby, in certain schools, faculty members specialise in providing tailor-made educational programmes for particular organisations after preliminary diagnosis of the problems and needs of the organisation. The advantages of tailor-made programmes are as follows:

■ Development is focused on addressing the business needs of the organisation, hence allowing for more immediate application of learning in the workplace.

■ Participants' attention can be focused on understanding and, if possible, addressing the problems of the organisation in a safe setting – the classroom. If nothing else, the problems of the organisation, through discussion and analysis, could at least be more appreciated by its middle and junior management.

■ The safe setting of the classroom could be used as a place in which to identify, debate and work through the irritants and frustrations experienced in the work environment. As indicated in Chapter 6, of particular advantage is the end-of-course dinner, where the senior executive of the organisation come to talk to and listen to the programme participants. For participants to influence the members of the top team in a positive manner can be of particular benefit.

- Communicating the organisation's values, mission and strategy, directly and indirectly through the programme content and the informal, out-of-class discussions, strongly reinforces the efforts of top management in the workplace. Highlighting the values and mission of the organisation in a development-oriented environment requires that top managers be confident of the value and sincerity of such statements, for, without question, intensive scrutiny will take place. At least, top managers would quickly know whether their mission statement does hold meaning. Managers on courses tend to tell their bosses pretty quickly what they really think.

Tailoring programmes can be undertaken on behalf of one client organisation as well as for specific industries or functions through the mechanism of consortia. Consortia are a form of joint development activity, whereby companies for particular reasons come together to organise their own training and development experience, with the assistance of a management-education institution. Managers, through sharing problems, discussing alternative approaches to solving problems, and being jointly trained by a business school faculty, seem to gain as much as individual managers attending general management programmes.

Another form of joint development activity is *action learning*, ie bringing together staff and management who need to solve problems, learn about particular concerns, or simply address issues, by acting together to improve matters. Action learning is exactly what the term states – learning from action – a method founded by Professor Reg Revans in the 1950s, simple in theory, but exceptionally powerful in practice. A number of organisations have exposed themselves and their managers to action learning, even at relatively senior levels; Thorn EMI is one company which has utilised the expertise of the consultant Dave Francis to facilitate the initiative throughout the organisation.

Furthermore, organisations are developing their own in-house expertise for training, development facilitation and consultancy. A number of mid- to large-sized corporations have well-organised, up-to-date internal training establishments providing company-relevant programmes. Certain organisations spend considerable time and effort on R & D in order to provide added-value programmes which directly attempt to influence job-related performance. The two banks discussed in this book provide examples of the best practice in terms of internal training and development. Vincent Dooley, Chief Training and Development Manager, Bank of Ireland, Retail Banking Division, probably spends as much, if not more, of his time, with colleagues in sales, marketing and line management as he does with his own training people, trying to understand the nature of the problems, and skills required to overcome particular problems, in order to focus training to address work-related concerns. Their recent review of staff attitudes, skills training and development within the division, highlights the bank's commitment to the development of its staff.

The NatWest Bank has introduced an interesting training innovation. Championed by John Fricker, Director of Group Training, the new programme, Essential Management Skills (EMS), was born out of integrating a number of separate programmes into one, in order to meet the needs of middle management. Planning for EMS started in 1987, the first programme ran in January 1988, and by the end of 1990 it had trained 7,500 junior and middle managers. Through the group's staff college, Heythrop Park, and through 31 regional centres, with additional facilities available in Ireland and New York and through Coutts & Co, which is also part of the NatWest group, it is expected that approximately 10,000 personnel will be trained through EMS over a five-year period. From there on, training will continue on an ongoing basis at Heythrop. NatWest's belief in training and its desire to have its management matured for responsibility and talking the same language, has led to one of the largest successful in-company training exercises in the UK. The participants in EMS, as well as their bosses, rate the programme highly.

Presentation skills

As managers are promoted to higher positions in the organisation, they have to make public presentations more often, not only to their own staff but also to outside public groups, and possibly on television. There is therefore a need to be skilled in making presentations. Speaking to a few people at an informal gathering is different from formally speaking to over 100 persons. Speaking in a lecture theatre is not the same as speaking on television. Being able to handle difficult questions put by news reporters or television interviewers is not the same as responding to questions or making presentations in the boardroom. All these are particular skills that need to be learned. Increasingly, senior managers are taking these matters seriously, for the standing of their organisation depends heavily upon the quality of their presentations in these various media. It is noticeable, therefore, how many chief executives undergo training on television presentation, learning how to convey their message without seeming to be defensive or caught off guard.

Personal development time

Senior managers should not underestimate the amount of training they need. The world changes fast. It is easy to become out of date. It is recommended, therefore, that senior managers establish a policy governing their own training similar to that established for personnel elsewhere in the organisation. Just as the finances of a business have to be budgeted for, so should time for training and development. It is sensible for senior managers to allocate at least five per cent of their time to attending external conferences and courses and keeping up to date with new issues. If they are in an industry that is subject to rapid change, such as many of the hi-technology industries, then this percentage may need to be as high as ten.

BEST PRACTICE INVENTORY

Dos

☐ Make feedback a part of training and development. Feedback can be focused at the individual level through tests and exercises. Feedback can be offered to teams. An essential part of feedback is the availability of counsellors to talk through the findings and their implications for individuals and teams.

☐ Respect the appraisal process. Appraisal, in reality, is an ongoing process of feedback. More often than not, the best form of appraisal is a blank sheet of paper between two people who are talking to each other. The results of their discourse can then be written down.

☐ Use consultants. Making the best use of consultants requires knowing how to utilise a consultant input. Do you want consultants to provide an expert input or to offer a facilitation service, or a combination of both? Making the best use of consultants will test your abilities as a client!

☐ Generate a human-resources strategy that helps managers become high achievers. Attention needs to be given to the breadth and depth of experience to which managers are exposed. Providing for early leadership experience is an important part of the development process.

☐ Develop a strategy for training. Consider which managers should be sent on external courses and which courses. A certain amount of shopping around is necessary in order to appreciate which business schools and other training establishments offer programmes best suited to the needs of your managers. In addition, the facility for tailor-made programmes is available at the better business schools or training establishments.

☐ Be prepared to rethink the training that is available within the organisation. It is becoming an increasingly common practice to

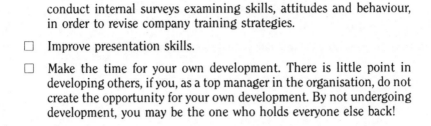

conduct internal surveys examining skills, attitudes and behaviour, in order to revise company training strategies.

☐ Improve presentation skills.

☐ Make the time for your own development. There is little point in developing others, if you, as a top manager in the organisation, do not create the opportunity for your own development. By not undergoing development, you may be the one who holds everyone else back!

The development of an organisation's management is crucial to the long-term success of that organisation. It is the top managers who identify the activities to be pursued, and the objectives to be achieved. It is they who create the conditions within which agreed targets are to be met.

Middle and senior managers need development so that they can appreciate the impact of what they are doing and why. On-the-job development needs to be considered in conjunction with off-the-job training. Feedback and being taught – ie emotional and cerebral learning – provide the tools for making full use of discretion in role, for understanding how to stimulate ownership of policies and actions, for appreciating how to combine pragmatism (costs and sales figures) with higher-order thinking (marketing, strategy, mission), and for having the patience, tolerance and insight to recognise how a less-than-disciplined senior executive can cause harm. Well-executed executive development provides learning at both the thinking and feeling level, so that managers can appreciate the complex relationship between high finance, market forces, and personal ego.

It is strange to report that in today's world of measurement, scientific rigour, and information technology, organisations and, in fact, the wealth-creation process are as much driven, or inhibited, by personal views and emotions, as by economic and market trends. You will never know until you enter a particular organisation whether it is emotion or concepts that are really driving that business. Under such unpredictable circumstances, it is best that you know what you are doing.

Appendices

Appendices

Appendix A: Earlier Research Leading to the Top Executive Survey

For the Cranfield team, research on senior managers began in the late 1970s through four studies: a study of UK CEOs (Margerison 1980), a study of CEOs in the US (Margerison and Kakabadse 1984), and two studies of middle-ranking and senior police officers (Kakabadse 1984; Kakabadse and Dainty 1988). The key findings from these studies are summarised in Table A.1.

Table A.1 *Characteristics of successful top managers*

- Drive and ambition to succeed
- Create their own opportunities
- Utilise mentors well
- Need to be flexible
- Need to be resilient
- Variety of personality types succeed
- Use different styles
- Work hard
- Considerably interact with people (stressor)
- Majority have business background of sales/marketing/ finance
- Majority exhibit broad experience of the various functions of the business

---

The key factor to emerge is that drive and ambition to succeed are paramount. The CEO's urge to attain high office and perform successfully in it is an important concern. People such as this display low dependency needs and thereby tend to create their own opportunities. One particular mechanism for such creation is to nurture relationships with influential people who can provide openings and chances for the individual to attempt a further challenge – successful managers indicated that they utilised mentors well.

A manager, driven to succeed and aware of opportunities, is likely to exhibit flexibility of style, in order to adjust to the different demands he faces. However, to cope with ambiguity, change and discontinuity, the manager requires considerable personal resilience in order simply to soak up pressure and proceed forward.

One interesting finding in these earlier studies is that no one personality type was linked to attaining or successfully maintaining high office. A reliable and respected psychometric assessment tool indicated no relationship between success (attaining and holding high office) and personality.* In fact, in contrast to the research on personality attributes, successful CEOs exhibited considerable adaptability in extending their portfolio of styles to suit circumstances. It was not personality that emerged as an influence on management style, but rather the individual's reading of a situation as to what approach should be used, when, and with what result.

Capacity for hard work and the energy to maintain concentration and momentum for long periods emerged as typical characteristics. Likewise, virtually all CEOs stated that they had much need for interpersonal skills in various situations, ranging from chairing meetings, holding informal discussions, meeting clients, and socialising. Although the volume of work may have been demanding, what, for some, turned strain into the more debilitating stress was the strain of interpersonal relations. Poor-quality relationships, a feeling of being undermined, and being overconcerned with how particular views or sentiments should be expressed, bearing in mind the sensitivities among senior managers, after a while tended to erode the morale and positive inclinations of CEOs. For some, such strain insidiously stretched into stress, and prevented them from fully contributing.

Finally, a majority of CEOs indicated that a broad experience of the different functions of the business is an important element of on-the-job development. Such experience is crucial in understanding the current and potential contribution of each function and how such a cost base can be fully utilised to enhance existing or future revenue streams.

These results, although interesting, did not satisfy the research team, for the competencies required in order to perform effectively at the top of organisations had not been succinctly identified and defined. What had

* The test used extensively was the Myers Briggs Work Preference Indicator.

emerged were individually oriented attributes, such as drives, style and flexibility – but not what you had to do to get there and stay there! After some deliberation, the research team recognised that a different approach to research on top managers was required. In order to identify the competencies required to induce high-level performance from top managers, why examine only CEOs? The *whole* of the executive needs study, in order to discover the views and positions adopted by each member of the executive, how issues are discussed, how ideas are generated, how decisions are made, and how effectively implementation of those decisions is undertaken.

For this reason, we invested time and effort on intensive and, at times, prolonged case studies of the *top team* and the levels of management below in order to discover what was really happening in organisations and what specifically distinguished effective from mediocre leadership.

It rapidly became apparent that the decision to undertake case-study analysis was right, for the simple reason that whatever the chairman/ CEO reported did not necessarily concur with the statements and views of others occupying a strategic role or general-management position. Differences of view are understandable, but when coupled with animosity, or a lack of understanding of the reasons why a colleague has adopted a different position, or even simple ignorance that a senior colleague holds a different view, then any one or more of these factors can engender a situation where lack of trust among senior management sets in and all too easily becomes a way of life until, like anything left neglected, it goes beyond repair. The isolation of a senior manager, the inability effectively to decide or act, and the feelings of frustration that can cloud judgement and eventually lead to staff turnover or simple underutilisation of talent, quickly and obviously become apparent in poorly managed organisations.

From the case studies, it became obvious that competence at senior levels needs to be examined within the context of the *senior executive*. The way in which the members of the senior executive relate, the manner in which they discuss key issues, and the styles they utilise to communicate and win the confidence of others, not only affect the *culture* of their team, but also directly affect the success of the business. In order to explore this fundamental insight, the Top Executive Survey was undertaken with a view to identifying categorically what senior managers need to do to ensure the successful and continuing existence of their organisation. It is the findings from the Top Executive Survey that have provided the data for this book.

Earlier research*

Considerable attention has been focused on top executives. However, the variety of viewpoints and interpretations adopted is considerable, including analyses of performance (Hackman 1984; Garfield 1986), effectiveness as a person and in role (Reddin 1970; Morse and Wagner 1978; Stewart and Stewart 1980), successfully attaining and maintaining high office (Mardique and Hayes 1985; Bradford and Cohen 1984); managerial competence (Byrd 1987; Taylor and Lippitt 1983; Starbuck and Miliken 1988), managerial behaviour (Dubin 1982; Whitely 1985), personality (Kets de Vries and Miller 1986), managerial work (Mintzberg 1980), leadership (Karmel 1978; Bolt 1985; Peters and Austin 1985), decision making (Shirley 1982; Shrivastava and Mitroff 1984), and organisational strategy and culture (Ohmae 1982; Chaffee 1985).

Although one needs to acknowledge such a spread of literature on the topic of the top manager, it is also necessary to indicate that the emphasis in each of these separate avenues has been towards the generation of theory rather than pragmatic application. There have been usable outcomes from certain studies (Blake and Mouton 1964; Reddin 1970), but even these have concentrated on developing training tools, rather than specifying the key skills areas to be developed for those who exhibit top executive potential.

* For a full account of the literature, see the Alderson and Kakabadse (1990) literature review.

Appendix B: The Survey Participants

The case studies involved extensive personal interviews with chairmen, CEOs and other senior directors/GMs, followed by consultancy, training, counselling or even further interviews with managers from lower levels. More than 480 top managers in the UK, Ireland, other European countries and the US were involved in both the interview and consultancy processes. Such an *action research* perspective involved the Cranfield team spending with certain organisations, at one end of the spectrum, only two to three weeks, whereas with others, well over three years of close and consistent dialogue and intervention was undertaken. We were there as much to offer support and facilitate pathways forward, as consultants, as we were on a voyage of discovery as researchers.

The detailed questionnaire survey that followed, involved 716 top managers. No distinction was made in the questionnaire between men and women, as the case studies strongly indicated that effective perform-ance was not in any way dependent upon gender. A greater spread of size of company is represented in the survey (Table B.1) than in the case studies. The case studies focused on business organisations of at least 2,000 employees, the largest employing approximately 120,000. However, 158 companies with over 2,500 personnel are represented in the survey.

Table B.1 *Company size*

	Number
< 100 employees	265
100–499	182
500–2,499	111
> 2,500 employees	158

A cross section of industries is represented in the survey: manufacturing (consumer), manufacturing (industrial), merchandising, transportation, financial services, management consulting, construction, industrial and product design, and educational and training services (Table B.2). An equal spread of companies from different industrial sectors formed the case-study sample, with emphasis on hi-tech manufacturing, industrial manufacturing, banks, publishing, management consultants, and information and communication services, as well as public-sector organisations such as police organisations, local authorities, and health-service organisations.

Table B.2 *Participant response – industry classification*

	Number	Percentage
Manufacturing (consumer)	125	17.5
Manufacturing (industrial)	226	31.6
Merchandising/wholesale/ retail	120	16.8
Transportation/distribution	89	12.4
Utilities	13	1.8
Financial/insurance	87	12.2
Medical/health care	27	3.8
Publishing	29	4.1
Government	10	1.4
Management consulting	71	9.9
Non-profit-making (service)	14	2.0
Other services*	232	32.4

* Other services include industrial/product designers, construction, and educational and training services

Just over 50 per cent of the respondents were employed in corporate HQ, whereas the remainder occupied strategic roles at divisional or subsidiary level (Table B.3).

Table B.3 *Work location*

	Number	Percentage
Corporate HQ	391	54.6
Division	126	17.6
Subsidiary	154	21.5
Other	45	6.3

Just under 60 per cent of the sample held the role of chairman/president/ CEO, with the least number of respondents being GMs (Table B.4). In the case studies, the role-position profile of respondents is skewed in the opposite direction, as there may be only one chairman, one CEO/MD, one president, but numbers of directors and GMs in any one organisation.

Table B.4 *Role position*

	Number	*Percentage*
Chairman/CEO/president	420	58.7
Director level	175	24.4
GM	121	16.9

There is a proportionate spread of responses on time spent in the company and on time spent in present job (Tables B.5 and B.6).

Table B.5 *Time spent in the company*

	Number	*Percentage*
< 5 years	186	26.0
5–10 years	169	23.6
11–20 years	205	28.6
> 20 years	150	20.9
Missing cases – 6		

Table B.6 *Time spent – present job*

	Number	*Percentage*
< 1 year	92	12.8
1–2 years	141	19.7
3–4 years	135	18.9
5–10 years	177	24.7
> 10 years	164	22.9
Missing cases – 7		

The respondents by age, fall mainly in the 36–55 bracket, with understandably, the lowest number being those under 36 years of age (Table B.7).

Table B.7 *Age of respondents*

	Number	*Percentage*
< 36	78	10.7
36–45	270	38.1
46–55	266	37.2
> 55	103	14.0

Sixty-two per cent of senior managers in this sample held a degree or professional qualification (Table B.8). In contrast, the Margerison and Kakabadse (1984) survey of US CEOs, identified 86 per cent of a sample of 712 top managers, as holding at least one degree.

Table B.8 *Educational experience*

	Number	*Percentage*
None*	24	3.4
School**	209	29.2
Undergraduate	243	33.9
Postgraduate	203	28.4

   * School leaving age < 15 years
 ** School leaving age > 15 years, ie possessing GCSE or 'A' levels
    Missing cases – 37

REFERENCES

Alderson, S and Kakabadse, AP (1990) 'Top Executive Development', Internal Cranfield Research Paper, Cranfield School of Management, SWP 12/91

Blake, R and Mouton, JS (1964) *The Managerial Grid*, Gulf Press, Houston

Bolt, JF (1985) 'Tailor executive development to suit strategy', *Harvard Business Review* (November–December), pp. 168–76

Bradford, DL and Cohen, AR (1984) *Managing for Excellence – The Guide to Developing High Performance in Contemporary Organisations*, Wiley, New York

Byrd, RE (1987) 'Corporate leadership skills – a new synthesis', *Organisational Dynamics*, vol. 16, iss. 1, pp. 34–43

Chaffee, EE (1985) 'Three models of strategy, *Academy of Management Review*, 10, No. 1 (January), pp. 89–98

Dubin, R (1982) 'Management – Meaning, methods and moxie', *The Academy of Management Review*, 7, no. 3 (July), pp. 371–9

Garfield, C (1986) *Peak Performers – New Heroes in Business*, Hutchinson Business, London

Hackman, JR (1984) *Doing Research that Makes a Difference*, Yale University Press,

Kakabadse, AP (1984) 'The police: a management development survey', *Journal of European and Industrial Training*, vol. 8, no. 5 (Monograph)

Kakabadse, AP and Dainty, P (1988) 'Police chief officers: a management development survey', *Journal of Managerial Psychology*, vol. 3, no. 3 (Monograph)

Karmel, B (July 1987) 'Leadership – a challenge to traditional research methods and assumptions', *The Academy of Management Review*, 3, no. 3, pp. 475–82

Kets de Vries, MFR and Miller, D (1986) 'Personality, culture and organisation', *The Academy of Management Review*, 11, no. 2 (April), pp. 266–79

Korn/Ferry International (1989) *21st Century Report: Reinventing the CEO*, a global study conducted jointly by Korn/Ferry International and Columbia University Graduate School of Business

McClelland, D (1965) 'Achievement motivation can be developed', *Harvard Business Review*, (November–December)

Mardique, MA and Hayes, RH (1985) 'The art of high-technology management', *The McKinsey Quarterly* (Summer), pp. 43–62

Margerison, CJ (1980) 'How chief executives succeed', *Journal of European and Industrial Training*, vol. 3, no. 3 (Monograph)

Margerison, CJ and Kakabadse, AP (1984) *How American Chief Executives Succeed: Implications for Developing High Potential Employees*, An AMA Survey Report

Mintzberg, H (1980) *The Nature of Managerial Work*, Prentice-Hall, Englewood Cliffs, NJ

Morse, JJ and Wagner, FR (1978) 'Measuring the process of managerial effectiveness', *Academy of Management Journal*, 21, no. 1 (March), pp. 23–35

Ohmae, K (1982) *The Mind of the Strategist – The Art of Japanese Business*, McGraw-Hill, New York

Parker, C and Lewis, R (1980) 'Moving up – how to handle transitions to senior levels successfully', *Cranfield School of Management Occasional Paper*

Peters, T (1988) *Thriving on Chaos*, Macmillan

Peters, T and Austin N (1985) *A Passion for Excellence – The Leadership Difference*, Collins, London

Reddin, WJ (1970) *Managerial Effectiveness*, McGraw-Hill, New York

Saxon Bampfylde International (1989) *The Search for the Euro-Executive*, Special Report, Old Queen Street, London

Shirley, RC (1982) 'Limiting the scope of strategy – a decision-based approach', *Academy of Management Review*, 7, no. 2 (April), pp. 262–8

Shrivastava, P and Mitroff, I (1984) 'Enhancing organisational research utilisation – the role of decision makers' assumptions', *Academy of Management Review*, 9, no. 1, pp. 18–26

Starbuck, WH and Miliken, FJ (1988) 'Executives' perceptual filters: what they notice and how they make sense', in: Hambrick, DC (ed.), *The Executive Effect: Concepts and Methods of Studying Top Managers*, *Strategic Management Policy and Planning*, vol. 2, JAI, Connecticut

Stewart, V and Stewart, A (1980) *Managing the Manager's Growth*, Gower, Aldershot, UK

Taylor, B and Lippitt, G (eds) (1983) *Management Development and Training Handbook*, McGraw-Hill, London

Whitley, W (June 1985) 'Managerial work behaviour – an integration of results from two major approaches', *Academy of Management Journal*, 28, no. 2, pp. 344–62

Index